CAPITALISM, SOCIALISM, ECOLOGY

CAPITALISM, SOCIALISM, ECOLOGY

ANDRÉ GORZ

Translated by Martin Chalmers

Afterword by Otto Kallscheuer

VERSO
London • New York

Published by Verso 2012
© Verso 2012
First published by Verso 1994
Afterword © Otto Kallscheuer 1991
Translation © Martin Chalmers 1994
First published as *Capitalisme, Socialisme, Écologie*
© Éditions Galilée 1991

3 5 7 9 10 8 6 4 2

Verso
UK: 6 Meard Street, London W1F 0EG
US: 388 Atlantic Ave, Brooklyn, NY 11217
www.versobooks.com

Verso is the imprint of New Left Books

ISBN-13: 978-1-78168-026-1

British Library Cataloguing in Publication Data
A catalogue record for this book is available from the British Library

Library of Congress Cataloging-in-Publication Data
A catalog record for this book is available from the Library of Congress

Typeset by Solidus Ltd, Bristol
Printed in the United States

Contents

Preface

As a system, socialism is dead. As a movement and an organized political force, it is on its last legs. All the goals it once proclaimed are out of date. The social forces which bore it along are disappearing. It has lost its prophetic dimension, its material base, its "historical subject"; History and the technical changes that are leading to the extinction, if not of the proletariat, then at least of the working class, have shown its philosophy of work and history to be misconceived.

Between 1961 and 1988, the size of the industrial working class shrank by 44 per cent in Great Britain, 30 per cent in France, 24 per cent in Switzerland and 18 per cent in West Germany. In the space of twelve years (1975–86), one-third or even half of all industrial jobs have disappeared in several European countries. During those twelve years, French industry did away with almost as many jobs as it created between 1890 and 1968.[1]

During the same period, a great number of jobs have been created in the service sector; but these are often part-time and/or precarious, low-skilled jobs, which offer no opportunities for career development and bear no relation to what constituted the essence and value of work and the workers in socialist doctrine. It is as though the industrial working class had declined and been partially supplanted by a post-industrial – largely female – proletariat which, by dint of the precariousness of its condition and the nature of its tasks, cannot derive from its work either a social identity or a mission to wield economic, technical or political power.

In short, work has changed, and the "workers" have changed too. We may ask what proportion of the workforce would still define their identity in terms of their work and their working lives. Or what proportion still regard their work as the focus of their lives. France is one of the rare countries that exhibits no desire to answer these questions: no newspaper or magazine, polling institution, trade union, employers' organization, ministry or university research centre carries out studies into the way attitudes to work are changing, or into ideas about work and life. I shall therefore take the results of the most recent survey published in West Germany, where, it must be remembered, industrial relations and working conditions are notoriously better than in France: only for 15 per cent of those questioned (35 per cent of senior managers) did their professional life still take priority over their personal life. For the immense majority, their work is no longer their life. It is no longer either qualitatively or quantitatively the focus of their life.

From the quantitative point of view, working lives are beginning later, ending earlier and being interrupted more frequently; at the same time, *annual, full-time* working hours fell from 2,150 in 1960 to 1,650 in 1990, and a further 150 hours can be deducted from this figure for sick leave. This amounts to a 23 per cent reduction in individual, annual, *full-time* working hours over a thirty-year period. Now, during those thirty years (I am still using the German figures), the annual volume of work (i.e. the total number of hours worked by all the members of the workforce) fell by 28 per cent, whilst production per hour of work increased threefold, and unemployment – or, rather, the impossibility of "earning a living" – assumed disquieting proportions.

What, in these conditions, is a Left perspective? What does it mean, in these conditions, "to be a socialist"? If it means fighting for the emancipation of the *workers*, then socialists are merely the elitist ideological spokespersons for those 15 per cent who still define themselves chiefly by their work, who feel they are workers first and foremost, and experience their work as an activity that is at least potentially fulfilling and creative. But should not socialism precisely make *all* work a creative and fulfilling activity? I certainly agree that it should be so, provided that we do not forget that "employment" – paid, productive work – occupies a proportion of our time (less than one-fifth of our waking lives) which is declining ever more rapidly, and that unpaid activities – whether necessary or freely chosen, private or social – cannot, in all honesty, be equated with that "work" on which the consciousness of belonging to the working class was built – the awareness of having interests, as a worker, which are opposed to those of capital.[2] Not all work is work in the same sense of the term. Not all work is a source of social identity or class belonging.

In these conditions, how are we to understand the future place of employment in the life of individuals and society? What is the future for a civilization whose increasingly efficient technologies create more and more wealth with less and less labour? Can we exit from the wage-based society without society as such being riven by antagonisms between an increasingly opulent group of privileged individuals and an ever-growing number of social outcasts. Can the wage-based society be saved by increasing the number of jobs which the founding fathers of political economy termed unproductive? Can it be saved by indefinitely continuing to monetize, professionalize and turn into paid occupations even the most basic daily activities? Or do we not have to find a source of activity and mode of social integration to replace wage-labour? Must we not go beyond the society of full employment and plan for a "full activity" society in which each person's income is no longer the price for which they *sell* their labour?

Does not this exit from the wage-based society throw capitalism itself, as an economic and social system, into question? Is it not for want of being formulated, comprehended, taken in hand by a political project, that such a questioning takes the negative form of disorientation, of an absence of perspective, a sense of insecurity and emptiness? Does it not seem more urgent than ever, now that the Soviet model has collapsed, to get beyond capitalism to a society in which the economic values of efficiency, profitability and competitiveness cease to be dominant, to a society which *makes use of* the economy for its own higher ends instead of being forced to serve it?

The term "socialism" no longer refers to any existing *social order*, nor even to any *model of society* that can be brought into being in the long or short term. Does this mean, then, that the socialist perspective and the reference to socialism have lost all meaning? Can we forget that capitalism dominates the world economy without needing to offer the world a social *order* or *model* of society? Can we allow ourselves to forget that our societies *are* capitalist societies, and that socialism does not need to define itself in terms of another social system existing elsewhere: it defines itself as opposition to capitalism – that is, as a radical critique of forms of society in which the social balance of forces, decision-making processes, technology, work, structures of everyday life, patterns of consumption and models of development all bear the stamp of a concern for the greatest possible profitability.

Abandoning the reference to socialism would lead also to abandoning any reference to a desirable "beyond" of capitalism, would lead us to accept this latter as "natural" and unchangeable, and to speak with a naive idealism of democracy and justice whilst treating as a negligible quantity the economico-material matrix of capital which, because it necessarily demands profitability above all, cannot help but be a source of domination, alienation and violence.

So long as we have no other term by which to refer to the transcending of capitalism (a transcending which must not be confused with the abolition of capital – a point to which I shall return below), the reference to socialism will have to be retained – on condition, however, that we redefine it. Jürgen Habermas argues along these same lines when he writes that socialism as "radical-reformist self-criticism of capitalist society . . . will only disappear when the object of its criticism disappears" – that is to say, "when the society being criticized is transformed to the point where it will be able to grasp the importance of, and take seriously, all those things that cannot be expressed as a sale or purchase price".[3]

Notes

1. On this question, see Emmanuel Todd, *L'invention de l'Europe*, Paris 1990.

2. See Chapters 6, 7 and 8 below.

3. Jürgen Habermas, "Was heisst Sozialismus heute?", in Habermas (ed.), *Die nachholende Revolution*, Frankfurt-am-Main 1990, p. 203.

1

Disorientations,

Orientations:

In Defence of Modernity

1. The so-called "real socialist" systems have collapsed. The Cold War is over. The West has won. Over whom? And over what? Is the West's victory a victory for democracy? A victory for capitalism? Can we now look confidently to the future and say that our social system has proved itself solid and durable; that it offers humanity the hope of a solution to its present and future problems; that it may serve as a model?

Is not its – relative and partial – superiority related rather to its instability, its diversity, its capacity to develop, to transform itself, to put itself in question, which features relate, in their turn, to its multiple internal contradictions, its complex, multiform character, comparable to that of an ecosystem, which continually triggers new conflicts between partially autonomous forces that can neither be controlled nor placed once and for all in the service of a stable *order*?

What is this complex society developing, changing and differentiating itself into? Is it moving towards thousands of partial markets that are increasingly less transparent, controllable or governable? Or is it going in the opposite direction, towards full social control of the forces and logic of the market? Or in both directions at once, in a process of whirls and eddies? Or in no discernible direction at all – towards a meaningless disorder, a chaotic barbarism (like many giant North or South American cities)?

Can a society perpetuate itself without direction or orientation, without any aim or hope. Can it perpetuate itself when the economic performance and efficiency which are its permanent obsession have as their supreme goal an excess of comfort? Will not a growing number of men and women be tempted, then, to seek a refuge from this absence of hope and orientation in abstractly religious – if not, indeed, fundamentalist – systems of thought?

1

After the outbreak of the Gulf War, the strongest wave of neo-pacifism for ten years swept through Europe – including, on this occasion, France. "No blood for oil," "Never again," "Peace now," "Immediate ceasefire," "Not a penny for arms" and "US go home" were some of the slogans – together with, on a giant banner carried by Hamburg school students, "*Wir haben Angst*" [We are scared]. Scared of what, of whom, and since when? Scared of a bloody tyranny which, with the support of its SS and Gestapo, following the precise pattern of the Nazi state, had clothed its policy of forced modernization in a garb of racism, militarism and conquest? Scared of Europe's inability to come out from under the shadow of the United States to carry out, with its own (diplomatic, economic and military) means, a global policy of its own which might respond to the desire of the peoples of the South for emancipation? Scared of the ease with which the alternative Left, the Greens, the Communists and the extreme Right were able to join in a common front with the neo-pacifists to denounce American imperialism alone as the enemy of humanity, freedom and peaceful coexistence? Or scared that peace will be saved by making concessions and showing leniency to an army of torturers and plunderers? On the basis of what common values was it possible, then, for a front to be formed running from Chevène-ment to Le Pen, from the alternative Left to the Club de l'Horloge, from the Greens to the PCF, from the Fourth International to the historic Gaullists?

2. The West is victorious; there is no other economic system but capitalism. The poor people of Central and Eastern Europe have for decades longed for nothing else. They thought that with the collapse of "real socialism" they would enter the realm of freedom, prosperity, security and justice. They had rushed to vote for the Right, believing that the Right represented conservatism, security, individual well-being, and social and moral order based on traditional values. But they were wrong: the Right represents the market, competition, productivist imperatives, lust for profit and love of gain; it represents letting the weakest go to the wall, dismantling social security and the public services, unemployment for a third – and soon, perhaps, for half – of the workforce of the former GDR, among others. They have, admittedly, been delivered from the totalitarian order, which is all well and good, and now they have freedom – but "freedom to do what?"

Capitalism cannot abide a stable social order. This was already stated in the *Communist Manifesto*: "All that is solid melts into air"; whatever resists change will be pitilessly swept away. Security, stability and salvation can be only imaginary, mythical or religious. The void left by the disappearance of the communitary social order rooted in tradition is filled by the nation, national sentiment and nationalism. The "identity" which has disappeared with this order can exist now only in the form of a self-affirmation without substance, of a "we are us": we are the Good, Evil comes from them; they are the ones to blame for the corruption of morals, the decadence of the nation, the disappearance of national–communitary cohesion. Let us protect ourselves from them; let us fashion from our identity the walls of an impregnable fortress.

In our part of the world, "they" are Turks, Pakistanis, Arabs, Jews, Jamaicans and Americans, whilst elsewhere "they" are Christians, Jews (again), Americans (again), Armenians and Kurds.... Forced modernization has prompted a flight into pre-modern, religious-nationalist ideologies and patterns of allegiance in Eastern Europe, in the Near and Middle East and in the South. But it is not only forced modernization that has done this. In the West, a modernization process begun three centuries ago – now accelerating with computerization, digitalization, fashion, the market, rap music, Instant Food, Instant Sex, the dissolution of all social bonds, of all forms of security, all patterns of allegiance, community, solidarity and stability – gives rise to the same escapist reactions.

In the eyes of radicals of both Left and Right, one country, one people symbolize all the perversions and ills with which "they" have corrupted the world. That country, the embodiment of the hated foreigner, the satanic Other, is "America", for America means "melting-pot", the loss of ethnic identity, the mixing of races and cultures, hypermobility, the disintegration of the traditional order, the decadence of elites and the decline of the higher values, the domination of rootless capital and the power of money, individuals left to their own devices with no safety net of social protection. "America" is ourselves as Other.

Nothing is closer to the nostalgic yearning of the religious fundamentalists and the extreme Right nationalists for an order which restores the unity of religion and life, work and morality, individual and national community, than the nostalgic aspiration on the extreme Left for a communitary society; nothing, in the eyes of both these groups, is more detestable than the emancipated individual, taking responsibility for his or her own life with a radically critical sense (whether Catholic or Protestant, Jewish or atheistic) of his or her autonomy. Ultimately, the enemy is, as ever, modernity – that is, the emancipation of individuals from the immutable obligations and fixed place assigned to them by the hierarchical social order.

I am not speaking here of the radical critique of American society and civilization, such as one finds in the work of Herbert Marcuse; nor of the struggle against US imperialism. What I am concerned with are the ideological presuppositions which, on both Right and Left, inflect that critique and that struggle towards a systematic denunciation on the basis of preconceived assumptions.

3. In the East, with the collapse of (un)real socialism, something else has also collapsed which has since been experienced there as a painful lack: the degree of moral comfort which a life regulated by a stable order – albeit an oppressive one – provides, together with the hope of seeing a different future, a future which, in another part of the world, was already a reality – our reality. I am referring to the reality of Western societies, which stands revealed to those who gain access to it as cruelly bereft of orientation, of perspective, of an openness to goals which it might be meaningful to pursue. Deep down, fear of the future, withdrawal into the private sphere and despair are not products of the hole in the ozone layer or the greenhouse effect, nor even of the justified fear of the unforeseeable consequences of – even a local – war. They are caused, rather, by this society's lack of a perspective and a project, and by the impossibility of continuing much longer with its way of doing things, its way of life – and not merely locally, but on a world scale. And they are caused by the collapse of social cohesion and lived social relations, the crisis of socialization, the fierce competition between job-hunters and, indeed, by all those things which render individuals impotent in the face of autonomized processes and faceless powers, and give rise to impotent protests and hatreds, to abstract glorifications of brute force, to nationalist-racist passions about identity or to finicky religiosities.

The reasons for this impotence are clearly to be found in the incomprehensible and insuperable complexity of a social system whose autonomized production machinery and processes pose a threat to the natural foundations of individual existence. But in saying this ("the system is wrong, it has to be torn up root and branch"), one has said nothing – at least, nothing of any political significance. For there is no different, transparently comprehensible, stable social system for which the real capitalist social system could be overthrown; nor does a historical subject exist that has the capacity to abolish it. The "global alternative" which communism once seemed to offer had already ceased to be credible by the 1950s – if, indeed, it ever had been.

With the final collapse of the Soviet system, however, it is not just a variety of socialism that has collapsed, a variety which – as may be demonstrated theoretically – could not be "truly socialist". What has also collapsed is the conception of "authentic" socialism (or communism) defined by the founding fathers, which continues to express itself in various ways in the form of a quasi-religious *faith*: the faith that it *must* be possible to get beyond this complex, opaque, differentiated, perpetually changing social system to recover the security and integration of pre-modern societies – that is, societies in which alienation (a term which, for the young Marx, refers to autonomized social forces turning, as inhuman powers, against individuals) is abolished; in which the unity of work and life, of society and community, of the individual and the collective, of culture and politics, of economy and morality, is re-established; in which the functional requirements of the system coincide with the aims of everyone, and the meaning of each person's life coincides with the meaning of History. In short, a society where state power, law, economic activity, the political sphere and culture would require neither distinct agencies nor institutions, since a just, stable, good order would have been instituted once and for all, with no possible further development: History would have reached its term, and the notions of progress and modernity would no longer have any meaning.

As I have attempted to demonstrate elsewhere,[1] in the Soviet case this unified, totally integrated society was to be built, in the form of the dictatorship of the proletariat, by total industrialization, and was to enable the individual to recognize him- or herself in the collectivity, to identify with the "collective productive worker", to feel at one with him. The undifferentiated unity of the social and the individual, of the economic, political, cultural and ethical spheres, as postulated by the system, openly came into contradiction, however – as might have been foreseen – with an industrialized economic apparatus which demanded differentiation, complexity, technical, geographical and professional specialization, the division of labour on a countrywide scale, exchanges between enterprises, and consideration of material needs and necessities in production decisions – in short, with the mechanisms of co-ordination, adjustment and equalization which, in the capitalist system, operate by way of markets and commodity relations between enterprises.

However, commodity relations and markets presuppose the relative autonomy both of the economic subsystem and of the management of economic units, the differentiation of the system into distinct (administrative, judicial, economic, political, scientific, etc.) spheres, and regulatory mechanisms which function according to their own laws independently of political power. All this is incompatible with an undifferentiated macro-social subject into which individuals are required to merge themselves totally.

The unity of communitary society, whether socialist or communist, presumes that the functioning of the social *system* can be controlled consciously and deliberately on the basis of the untrammelled, intuitive perceptions of lived experience and the needs or interests of all. In the case of an industrial system, this collective control was to be secured by Five-Year Plans. These were to render comprehensible a social machinery which was otherwise opaque by virtue of its size and complexity; and they were to translate overall system-level objectives into goals which everyone could espouse. Now, as ought to have been expected, the planned control by which the system as a whole was to become intuitively comprehensible itself demanded an administrative apparatus of an incomprehensible complexity which could not be mastered by individuals. That apparatus acquired autonomy *vis-à-vis* society and even *vis-à-vis* the agencies of government, pitting its own specific inertia against both decisions from above and initiatives from below. The autonomy of the economic subsystem from the experience and life of individuals, which in capitalism takes the form of market laws, here assumed the form of an autocratic and oppressive planning apparatus. This produced an alienation even more total than that of the market system, since, as it was not differentiated into spheres and institutions that could interact with relative autonomy, the Soviet system did not permit politico-administrative decisions to be adapted to real economic conditions or to felt needs. The system was bereft of a developmental dynamic of its own; it was incapable of reproducing – and hence unable to cope with – the degree of complexity and rate of innovation of capitalist industrial societies. It possessed both the failings of an immobile, pre-modern society and the defects of industrial capitalism, without having the advantages of either.[2]

4. These remarks are intended to indicate that a unified communitary society of a pre-modern type is impossible in the conditions of an industrial economy, which is necessarily complex. "Real" socialism demonstrated the inevitable failure of endeavours to re-establish the unity of life and reason in these conditions. A unified communitary (communist) society could be established (or re-established) only by reducing the complexity of the social system, a move which presupposes the "wholesale abolition" of industrial techniques and functional specialization – and of the subdivision of tasks and commodity exchanges they require – in favour of a stable social order (a stable-state economy) employing means of production that can be mastered by small communities for their own subsistence production.

This is precisely the "de-industrial" utopia of the most radical Greens. It is an updating, in regressive form, of the project of communist society. And since there is no social or historical subject capable of bringing this utopia into being, the theory of the inevitable collapse of capitalism is reworked in an ecological version (though one which is not wholly without verisimilitude). In that version, capitalist civilization is moving inexorably towards catastrophic collapse. There is no longer any need for a revolutionary class to overthrow capitalism: it is digging its own grave, and that of industrial civilization in general. The pre-modern character of this eco-radical theory is to be found in the way that it envisages the birth of a post-industrial society not as the result of a *development* by which capitalism would transcend itself, but as a destruction due to external factors. The dialectical materialist faith in a meaning and direction of history gives way to quasi-religious faith in the goodness of Nature, and of a natural order which is to be re-established.

There are thus more than incidental affinities between "Green" and religious fundamentalism. Indeed, we cannot entirely rule out Islamic fundamentalism resorting to biological or nuclear weapons in order to annihilate godless modern civilization with its own wicked technology. From the point of view of pre-modern fundamentalisms, the whole development of modernity, from its beginnings right up to our own day, has been a sin against the natural order of the world. Its catastrophic end will force humanity to make the necessary conversion. There is nothing to conserve, and nothing will remain. There is no rational path to salvation; only the inevitable collapse can open up the way.[3]

5. Yet it remains an open question whether there might not be a possible way forward, staking our hopes not on a return to the past but on the capacity of modern societies to transcend themselves and enter on a different mode of development from the one which has shaped them up to now. Is not this capacity for transcendence contained in the fundamental capacity for reform which modern social systems possess by virtue of the instability and mobility to which their complexity condemns them? Does not capitalism, which has hitherto been the only form of society capable of continual development and change, contain latent potentialities of liberatory transformation? Is that society capable of evolving *because* it is capitalist, or can it perhaps transcend its capitalist form *because* it is capable, by virtue of its modern complexity, of evolving? Are not modernization and the differentiation of spheres of activity and institutions incomplete so long as one of these spheres subordinates the others to its instrumental rationality – so long, to use Habermas's words, as "capitalist development . . . promotes a pattern of rationalization such that cognitive-instrumental rationality penetrates beyond the economy and state into other spheres of life and there enjoys a preeminence at the expense of moral-practical and aesthetic-practical rationality?"[4] Does not the development of modern society in the direction of ever greater differentiation demand that the domination of lived aspirations and

needs by economic rationality – that is, by the market, by exchange value, by the logic of capital – now be abolished? How are we to describe the import of this development which would abolish capitalism to the extent that it would limit the scope of the criteria of profitability and thus the power of capital, and would orientate the economy and technology – and hence the model of consumption – not towards the maximization of profitability but towards an optimum quality of life? Does not such a reorientation, with all that it implies in terms of the extension of democratic powers, correspond to the original, primal meaning of "socialism", a meaning which certainly should not be confused with its traditional historical contents?

Socialism is, without doubt, totally obsolete if it is reduced to its traditional contents: to the "full development of the productive forces"; to the collectivization (or socialization) of the means of production; to the appropriation and direct control of the means of production and exchange by the "associated producers"; to the planned management of the economic system conceived as a single large enterprise; to the abolition of wage-labour and commodity relations; to the suppression of the state and of the relative autonomy of the state administration, the judiciary, the press, art, the economy, the private sphere, and so on – in short, if it is reduced to the restoration of the pre-modern, undifferentiated unity of the individual, community and functional spheres of paid work and self-determined activities; a restoration which, breaking radically with the complexity of modern social systems, is intended to have a stable order as its end product.

If, on the other hand, the contents of the socialist projects of the past are viewed not in themselves but in their relationship with the conditions of the time, they still retain a clear meaning for us today. The objective was then, and – as I shall attempt to demonstrate below – still is today, to limit the field in which economic rationality may find expression – or, in other words, to limit the logic of profit and the market. The point is to subject economic and technical development to a pattern and orientations which have been thought through and democratically debated; to tie in the goals of the economy with the free public expression of felt needs, instead of creating needs for the sole purpose of enabling capital to expand and commerce to develop. But the social actors pressing for such a development are no longer, first and foremost, the rapidly declining class of industrial workers, even though their occupational and class organizations must continue to exert a decisive influence on the development and outcome of social conflicts.

6. The idea of a "reflexive evolution of the economy" – a concept

introduced by Rainer Land, echoing that of "reflexive modernization" proposed by Ulrich Beck – could present the most fertile approach for renewing and redefining socialism.[5] Rainer Land sees the fact of capital acquiring autonomy from felt needs as the prime condition for the dynamic of economic development, as I do too. Without the achievement of that autonomy, production would never have been able to go beyond what is perceived, in terms of traditional norms, as "enough"; it could never have had as its goal the accumulation of what Baran and Sweezy called an "economic surplus", the creation of endlessly expanding needs and continually reborn desires.[6]

"The fact of the social apparatuses of production becoming autonomous from individuals and the self-referentiality of those developmental forces are the preconditions *both* for the capacity of modern societies to evolve and for the destructiveness of the developmental tendency which is set in train within them," writes Land.[7]

> The system's regulatory mechanisms choose from among the potential innovations those which best permit the autonomized economic system to consolidate and reproduce itself. Technics and technology, ecology and transport systems, urbanization, towns and municipalities, and work all evolve in such a way as to ensure the growth and effectiveness of the autonomous production process, as indeed do housing conditions, styles of consumption, nutrition, family life, etc. . . .[8]

The object is always to satisfy needs with the greatest possible flow of commodities, to produce these with the techniques which permit of the greatest profit and, lastly, to accord prime importance to those needs which are most profitably satisfied.

The key question which an updated conception of socialism must pose can therefore be formulated as follows: how can the development of the economy be given a social and ecological orientation? How can that development be shaped and directed without, in the process, destroying the economy's relative autonomy and its capacity to evolve? The answer cannot simply be to eliminate the autonomized economic and social forces (of the state, capital, money, the market, the legal system). For though that elimination makes it possible to impose directly political objectives upon development, it leads just as directly to "the dead-end of the forms of bureaucratic-administrative society", which are just as incapable of adjusting their economic decisions to the needs and lifeworld interests of individuals. All Soviet-type systems, including the so-called "socialist" dictatorships of Africa and the Near and Middle East which have aspired to use the state apparatus to bring about their economic development, have proved incapable, for want of democratic feedback between grass roots and leadership – between demand and supply – to develop their own socialist model of consumption and pattern of work, and their own production techniques. They have been capable of employing or developing modern techniques only for unproductive purposes of prestige and power – purposes entirely foreign to the lived interests and aspirations of civil society. They have offered no alternative to the capitalist model of consumption and have become, in the end, mere caricatures of that model.

7. The problem to be resolved thus consists in preserving the relative autonomy of the state, culture, the legal system and the press, and so on – and also, indeed, of the economy – without surrendering the aim of shaping and orientating economic and technical development in a social-ecological direction. And, as Land stresses, we must also not forget that "the definition of the contents of development takes place only within the context of the effective process of innovation and selection", and that as a result, by seeking to predetermine these contents in the form of a pre-established plan, one "actually consolidates the existing structures" by "excluding structural change and qualitative transformations".[9] Only the general orientations of development – its priorities and particular goals – can be pre-established, and these may be contrary to strictly economic criteria (to the extent, for example, that they impose conditions on enterprises which increase their costs), but the precondition for these will always be an economy that is efficient enough for the potential surplus it produces to be redirected in large measure to non-economic ends.

> This does not mean plans are superfluous. However, their function is no longer to predetermine the contents of development, but rather to define the reproductive dimension. For it to be possible for development to be shaped and directed, the most important point is that processes of innovation and selection should be tied in to the aspirations and life interests of individuals, i.e. that procedures of political participation should be established which allow individuals to bring the "autonomized social machine" into line with – and place it in the service of – their life interests.... In a word, the aim must be to democratize economic decisions.[10]

Only by "establishing criteria of choice" can meaning be given to economic development – criteria by which it will be shaped and orientated in response to felt aspirations and within a framework of democratic procedures. "*It is in these processes that the as yet unexploited potential for the genuine transformation of capitalism into a new society lies.*" It is here, too, that "the true fields of historic action of the socialist movements – the real alternative to the administrative-bureaucratic social system" are to be found.[11]

This "connecting back" (which would be the literal translation of the systems theory term *Rückbindung*) of economic decisions to felt aspirations and needs obviously cannot be achieved by state intervention (even though such intervention is also indispensable).

> It is effective only when individuals organize themselves into countervailing powers ... while, at the same time, retaining their roots in their lifeworlds ...: even when they represent the life interests of individuals, organizations tend to become ossified and must constantly be renewed by protest and autonomous social movements. Alienation is not eliminated by destroying at a stroke the social forces which have acquired independence from human control ... by a Romantic return to premodern forms of society.[12]

"Such an elimination is to be achieved, rather, by the permanent action of countervailing powers" which, in complex social systems, will never eliminate the structures and powers of an inert social machinery once and for all. The split between society as a system and the untrammelled, intuitive perceptions of the lifeworld cannot be completely surmounted. All attempts to do away with alienation in complex societies by striving for the unity of system and lifeworld – of functional, heteronomous tasks and personal activity – have produced disastrous results.

> The conflict can be eliminated and resolved only by continually renewed mediations. The only solutions are provisional ones: once they have become institutionalized, the countervailing powers lose their effectiveness when the social movements on which they are based ebb away.[13]

I quote Rainer Land at length here because I find my own conclusions and intuitions reflected in the writings of this young East German teacher of political science.[14] He had first to rework, then to transcend, his Marxist philosophical training in the encounter with an unacceptable "real socialism" , and he found the intellectual armoury for that transcendence in the writings of Western philosophers (particularly Luhmann and Habermas), for whom it is clearly impossible to abolish complex social systems by a revolutionary frontal attack, but for whom it is also impossible to become reconciled with the megamachine those societies resemble. The solution (and I shall return to this several times in what follows) consists in winning from the megamachine (or the "system" , as Habermas calls it) broader and broader spaces in which a "logic of life" can unfold freely, and in making the system compatible –

by its orientations, its techniques, the limits of the space it occupies and the restrictions and rules to which its functioning is subject – with that free unfolding of life. This perpetual action of laying down orientations, of shaping and subjecting the system to a rationality which is not its own – that of the personal fulfilment of individuals – will never be finished. Socialism cannot and must not be conceived as an alternative *system*; it is, rather, nothing other than the transcendence of capitalism which social movements open up when they fight for a development modelled on people's lived needs, a development which connects with their aspirations and interests. That battle is never definitively won or lost. It continues, and it will continue.

8. I shall confine myself for the moment to a brief and partial enumeration of the pressing objective issues which determine the present contents of that struggle.

(i) The ecological restructuring of society demands that economic rationality be subordinated to an eco-social rationality. That subordination is incompatible with the capitalist paradigm of maximization of productivity and profit. It is also incompatible with a market economy which forces competing enterprises into constant product innovation and differentiation, into continually creating new desires and proposing satisfaction of those desires by raising consumption to as high a level as possible, into putting obstacles in the way of that self-limitation of needs which would be the effect of production for oneself and the "free choice" of working hours.

(ii) If the ecological restructuring of the economy is to be effected not by technocratic and authoritarian *dirigisme* but by the reconstitution of a lifeworld, the fall in the production of commodities and commodity services will have to be achieved by way of a self-limitation of needs experienced as a reconquest of autonomy – that is, by way of a democratic reorientation of economic development, with a simultaneous reduction of working hours and an extension, assisted by the creation of collective or community facilities, of the scope for co-operative or associative "own-use" production. Policies conceived along these lines must imperatively be thought out and implemented on a European scale, on the scale of a "European eco-social space". It is on this scale alone that commercial competition and commodity rationality can be subjected to restrictive rules. There can be no nationalist Left, nor any merely national perspective for socialism. "Will there be a European Left?" This is the question that has to be answered first, and it is confronted here by Otto Kallscheuer in the Postface to the present work.

(iii) "Socialism" should not be taken to mean merely subordinating the economy to the needs and values of society. It also involves the creation, as an effect of ever shorter and increasingly flexible working hours, of a growing sphere of sharing within the community, of voluntary and self-organized co-operation, of increasingly extensive self-determined activities. It is only by adopting such a course that the reduction in the amount of work required by the economic system will not simply lead to unemployment and the disintegration and South-Africanization of societies.

(iv) For such a policy of reduction in working hours to be able to redistribute both work performed for payment and the domestic work of self-maintenance, caring and child-rearing, income levels will have to cease to depend on the evolution of working time and the actual number of hours worked. The fact that a growing proportion of the workforce is already employed on tasks in which the productivity of labour is not measurable and that, for an increasing part of the active population, there are no regular or full-time jobs makes such an uncoupling all the more obviously imperative. The right to interrupt one's working life without loss of income, together with the right to "freely choose one's working hours" and to manage one's own hours of work, amount to emancipatory demands that are now achievable.

The right to an income uncoupled from length of working time does not need to be justified by the alleged "social utility" of the activities accomplished in the private household sphere. The argument that so-called "reproductive" activities or work in the private (and, in particular, family) sphere have a usefulness for society which is at least the equal of work in production masks a concern to rescue the ideology of work and utilitarianism peculiar to industrial societies. That utilitarianism is losing its validity and basis as technical developments are increasing the volume of disposable time. The point is to understand how and in what specific ways everyone – men and women – can take advantage of this disposable time; and this question, which is that of the very meaning of existence, transcends all calculations and criteria of utility. This is so because the criterion of utility always asks: "What purpose does it serve?" For what purpose *external* to itself is an activity useful? Disposable time, by contrast, time liberated from necessary work, acquires its meaning only in those activities which have no other end than their own unfolding: they are the time of life, the very unfolding of life itself.

JANUARY 1991

Notes

1. See A. Gorz, *Critique of Economic Reason*, London 1989, Part I, Chapter 4 (pp. 39–50).

2. The notions employed here are more precisely defined in Chapter 8 below, "Which Way is Left?".

3. A Green "fundamentalist", Jürgen Dahl, argued this conception in a particularly coherent way in his essay "Die letzte Illusion" [The last illusion] in *Die Zeit* 48, 23 November 1990, pp. 57–60. "It would be presumptuous", he concludes,

> to dare to predict where the weak point might lie from which the ... collapse will develop. The world ... is the victim of the opulence which has been enjoyed at its expense but, in falling victim to that opulence, ... it also renews itself and will regain a balance, though with fewer inhabitants, less beauty and less wealth. As a necessary consequence of the opulence, there will be great poverty.... Only poverty can save us ... enforced renunciation. And since no one will choose the state of poverty of his own free will while such wealth is easily to hand ... that poverty will have to come about as ineluctable fate.

4. Jürgen Habermas, *The Theory of Communicative Action*, vol. 1: *Reason and the Rationalization of Society*, trans. Thomas McCarthy, Boston, MA 1984, p. 233.

5. Rainer Land, "Ist wirtschaftliche Entwicklung gestaltbar?", in Michael Brie and Dieter Klein (eds), *Umbruch zur Moderne*, Hamburg 1991. Land, a teacher first of philosophy, then of political science, at the Humboldt University of Berlin (East), was until 1990 the central figure in an initially clandestine group of thinkers who met to discuss fundamental reforms to "real socialism" (see R. Land and M. Brie [eds], *Das Umbaupapier*, Berlin 1990). Land's thinking and vocabulary bear the stamp of Marx, Habermas and the systems theory of which Niklas Luhmann is the chief representative in Germany. On the concept of "reflexive modernization", see Ulrich Beck, *Risikogesellschaft*, Frankfurt-am-Main 1986.

6. Cf. *Critique of Economic Reason*, Part II, Chapter 9, pp. 109–26.

7. R. Land, "Evolution und Entfremdung. Wirtschaftliche Subsysteme und individuelle Lebenswelten in der gesellschaftlichen Entwicklung", *Initial* 6, Berlin 1990, pp. 636–47.

8. Land, "Ist wirtschaftliche Entwicklung gestaltbar?"

9. Land, "Evolution und Entfremdung ...".

10. ibid., pp. 643–4.

11. Land, "Ist wirtschaftliche Entwicklung gestaltbar?".

12. ibid.

13. Land, "Evolution und Entfremdung ...".

14. Cf. *Critique of Economic Reason*, Part I.

2

A Left in Need of

Redefinition

We are at this moment living through a cultural mutation, a great stirring up of social life in which the circulation of people, ideas and capital is more intense than before; but the exhaustion of the old ideas and programmes still weighs upon us and, though some intellectuals are already pointing out the realities and problems that are taking shape, most are turning into guardians of the outdated ideologies, if not indeed into scornful critics of the new ideas.

ALAIN TOURAINE

To the left of the entrance to his church, the bishop of Cuernavaca in Mexico had put up a notice bearing the following words: "There are the oppressors and the oppressed. Which side are you on?" For those who, today, ask themselves in what way the Left still differs from the Right – or even in what regard the Left–Right distinction still has meaning in Western societies – this evangelical summons offers not an answer, but a method: it states as axiomatic that every society is divided into two by a central conflict, and that no one can avoid being part of that conflict.

Yet this central conflict remains to be defined. Who are the oppressors and who are the oppressed, who are the dominators and who are the dominated, and what is at stake in the conflict between them? In Latin America the matter seems relatively simple. It is not immediately obvious in Western Europe and North America, where ideologies lag behind cultural, social and technical changes, and the political machines continue to fight over issues and on terrains which correspond less and less to the new dimensions of the conflict and its new stakes. As a result of this lag, it is not the opposition between Right and Left that is losing its pertinence, but the (media, party political) opposition between the political apparatuses which claim allegiance to one or the other. Increasingly, the real frontier between Left and Right does not run between these apparatuses but, rather, between the parties which occupy the institutional centre stage, on the one hand, and the movements rising up on their margins and contesting them, on the other. The established political organizations are falling into discredit, except where they succeed in incorporating, in a process of renovation, the themes with which the new social actors are now outflanking them.

The discredit into which the established political organizations are falling is clearly visible in all the developed countries, and the con-servative parties find themselves in a crisis more difficult in some respects to overcome than the one facing those who claim to be of the Left. The classical Right has, in effect, always been obliged to defend the power of the dominant class in the name of a conception of the general interest and the social order which transcends that class. In modern capitalist societies, it has to embody both the demands of capital – for maximum profitability and competitiveness, technical and economic modernization, domination of the process of reproduction and the orientation of development – and traditional values – family, work, fatherland, order and authority – which are constantly being under-mined by the logic of the commodity, expertocracy and the invasion of the life-milieu by megatechnologies.

Particularly in periods of radical change and accelerated technical innovation, capitalism breaks down the social order, shatters cohesion and "identities", sweeps away traditional norms and values, and dissolves those communities, allegiances and exchanges that were formerly felt to be entirely natural by bringing them under a system of technical constraints and legal formalization. This is what Habermas calls the "colonization of the lifeworld" by the "economic and administrative subsystems".

Besides prompting opposition from the Left (to which we shall return), this colonization of the lifeworld, this destruction of the intuitive patterns of interpretation and traditional ethical codes, gives rise to a *conformist revolt*, which the Right has at all costs to represent and channel, on pain of losing its social base. In a society undergoing complexification and radical change, the Right is thus faced with the difficult task of having to represent *both* aspirations for order, stability, security and the preservation of traditional cultural norms and concep-tions *and* the modernizing and expansionist demands which are causing capital, in order to satisfy its need for profit, to reshape spheres of activity and life formerly spared by commodity logic.

In consequence, the Right is constantly threatened with break-up. If it identifies too openly with the modernizing dynamic of capital, it will provoke the emergence on its Right of a traditionalist, populist conservative force. If, on the other hand, it identifies with the conservative resistance to modernization, it will give rise, in the best of cases, to a decadent, corporatist and immobilist state such as the Salazar or Franco regimes, or the Greece of the colonels.[1]

In the past, the Right could resolve its dilemma by supporting the modernizing strategy of capital in the name of an aggressive and conquering nationalism which to some extent compensated, by patriotically extolling the national community, for the dislocation of traditional systems of allegiance and life. We know that this solution has become impossible today. Far from being able to provide a cover for capitalist modernization (except, perhaps, in an imperial nation that was economically and militarily dominant on a planetary scale, an ambition which is becoming impracticable) and to compensate for it, the extolling of national grandeur, traditions and identity is today a form of resistance and reaction against that modernization, against the globalization of markets, capital and the division of labour. Chauvinism, racism, fundamentalism and xenophobia – which, in the past, could provide support for the imperial expansionism of a conquering national-capitalism – are today regressive reactions to an essentially technocratic and stateless capitalism. That capitalism cares nothing for traditional nationalism and military power. The weapons of its imperialism are technical advance, conquest of markets and information control. The Right is obliged to find themes which provide an outlet for conservative revolt while serving the cause of capitalist modernization. It found them first in Scandinavia, then in the USA, and then in the rest of Europe. They are fiscal revolt, anti-bureaucratic sentiment and the rejection of state interventionism.

These themes are interesting on account of their ambivalence. On the one hand, they quite clearly have a neo-liberal dimension of rehabilitating free competition in a free market between free individuals and free enterprises. They restore a positive role to an economic liberalism which, for more than a century and a half, has progressively been held in check by the labour movement and the social state. It was in that struggle to impose restrictive rules on the free workings of the market – which both permit and demand the maximization of efficiency and profit – and to define areas from which the market was excluded that the Left took shape and developed. Gradually, the Left has come to circumscribe more and more the space within which free competition and the pursuit of maximum productivity are given free rein. In other words, it has withdrawn from the rule of economic rationality larger and larger fields (such as health, education, housing, the family, old age provision, etc.) to which the priorities and criteria of the pursuit of maximum returns were not applicable.

The social state has, none the less, left intact the mode of operation of the economic system and the hegemonic dynamic of its type of rationality. The restriction of the sphere in which that rationality is allowed free rein is entirely dependent on strengthening the state's powers of intervention. Strengthening those powers has not given rise to a different public space, to other forms of sociality, other forms of life and work governed by an autonomous rationality and values. Thus the redistributive action and the regulatory interventions of the state have been regarded by their beneficiaries as representing "social gains", as a bureaucratic guardianship, and as the despoiling of the more "high-powered" for the benefit of the less able.

Habermas has described, on several occasions, how "an ever denser net of legal norms, of governmental and para-governmental bureaucracies is spread over the daily life of its potential and actual clients"; how "the lifeworld is regimented, dissected, controlled, and watched over" by "the professionalization and scientization of social services" and by "normalization and surveillance ... down to its very finest capillary ramifications in everyday communication"; he concludes: "the establishment of forms of life that ... open up arenas for individual self-realization and spontaneity ... cannot be reached via the direct route of putting political programs into legal and administrative form".[2]

In so far as it is based on the consolidated *domination* of daily life by normalizing and formalistic administrative bodies, the welfare state is as far as it could possibly be from the libertarian aspirations for individual and collective liberation which are one of the founding dimensions of the Left. Instead of expanding the power social individuals have over their lives, over the modes and outcomes of their social co-operation, the welfare state, running parallel in this with capital, subjects them to its own power and deprives them of their space of autonomy in exchange for the forms of security they are guaranteed. That is why "Today the [social-statist] legitimists are the true conservatives, who want to stabilize what has been achieved" by attempting to find "a point of equilibrium between the development of a welfare state and modernization based on a market economy ...". This type of programme "fails to recognize, however, the potentials for resistance accumulating in ... communicatively structured lifeworlds", made conscious of their fragility and autonomy by their "progressive bureaucratic erosion".[3]

It is easy to see how the Right can exploit this situation. With the established Left bogged down in a social-statism whose fiscal limits – and bureaucratic burdensomeness – are becoming evident, the Right can claim the inheritance of the Left's libertarian aspirations for a politics which dismantles the welfare state, lightens the fiscal burden, "de-regulates" and abandons the development of a complex society to market forces reputed to be "neutral" and "free" because they lie beyond the scope and conscious determination of human beings. To the Right's traditional social base this politics promises enhanced possibilities of social promotion and individual success ("effort" and "merit" will be better rewarded thanks to the reformed tax system); to the new salaried strata and to a not inconsiderable fraction of the skilled workers and technicians it offers the rehabilitation of success through work, within an alliance of "winners" – an alliance of "workers" and "entrepreneurs" against the "idlers" and "incompetents" who are seeking to live off the work of others by way of social benefits. The laws of the market demand efficiency and optimum performance; the competitiveness of the economy depends on that of each enterprise: "we are at war", and everyone has to be fired with "the will to win". A nation of winners cannot grieve over the fate of the weak or those who are unable to keep up; it will function all the better the more effectively it marginalizes these "new poor", from whom – as was not the case with the proletarian masses of the last century – it has nothing to fear and no benefit to derive, except perhaps in so far as they might provide cheap services for the most able.

In a context in which there can no longer be stable full-time jobs for all, this extolling of maximum effort and glorification of employment as a source of social identity and national wealth and greatness will succeed in clouding the political waters by disconcertingly overturning the previous system of allegiances: as a result, the class of skilled wage-earners with stable jobs will be induced to behave as *jealous proprietors* of that rare commodity, employment, and to ally with the traditional middle classes and the modern employers to defend their jobs and wages against the pressure from a growing mass of unemployed workers, both native and non-native, and from competing enterprises.

The ideology of effort and individual merit, the defence of jobs and identification with work, have thus become right-wing themes, enabling blocs of the working class to be won over to a new national-productivist alliance in favour of liberal-capitalist modernization. The old Left has seen a crucial part of its ideology and social base stolen by the Right. The terrains it occupied in the past are no longer rightly its own; they are no longer terrains of the Left. Hence the perplexity and scepticism regarding the pertinence of the Right–Left divide. Hence also the obvious fact that if there is a Left, it has to be sought on other terrains than those of national-productivism, the ideology of work, of the wage-earning society, of social-statism and a "collective utilitarianism", as Alain Caillé would put it, for whom collective well-being is to be achieved only by renouncing the autonomy of the subject.

It is in terms of this latter theme of the autonomy of the subject (in Marx's language, "the free development of individuality") that a Left political orientation has to be defined today. The question post-industrial societies face is, in fact, the question of *the use that will be made of the savings of labour* which ensue from the development of technologies. The conservative response, shared by the old Left and the various strands of the Right, consists in counting on the indefinite expansion of the sphere of waged and commodity activities to save the wage-based society and open up new fields of profitable investment for capital. We know that this is a solution that can be achieved only on the basis of a dual society, with well-paid wage-earners with stable conditions of employment in the highly capital-intensive sector, which produces the greater part of the economic surplus, and precarious and very low-paid workers in an increasingly extensive service sector which, culturally, presents the redhibitory defect of monetizing, economicizing, professionalizing and generally alienating from subjects the activities by which they produce and reproduce themselves, and by which they take control of their lives as autonomous existences.[4]

By contrast, the response which will henceforth define the Left, and by which the Left will define itself as such, consists in viewing the savings of working time as a *liberation of time*, by virtue of which social individuals should be able to emancipate themselves from the constraints of economic rationality embodied in capital (i.e. in the domination of dead over living labour). To emancipate themselves not by abolishing capital and the sphere of economically rational commodity activities (as the communist or fundamentalist anti-moderns or pre-moderns imagine), but by assigning them a limited and subaltern function in the development of society. In other words, the societal objective of productivity gains must be to bring about a contraction of the sphere governed by economic calculation and an expansion of the self-determined, self-organized spheres of activity in which human faculties can develop freely.

To use the potentialities of technology not to reinforce the domination of the apparatuses over people's lives, consumer choices and time, but to free social individuals from the constraints of the social mega-machine and increase their power over their own lives and the development of society – this is the alternative which today defines the Left–Right divide or, as Alain Touraine puts it, the "central conflict". This central conflict develops on many terrains and in multiple forms (one can easily imagine how it impacts upon international policy options regarding economic "co-operation" and "development"), all of which, however, share a "central stake, namely the use society will make of its own capacity to act upon itself"; the use it will make, in particular, of technology and "of the symbolic goods it produces in vast quantities". That stake is not entirely new. "Classes fight for ... the management of the means whereby society 'produces' itself.... The dominated class ... fights for a collective reappropriation" of those means.[5] What is new is that this dominated class is everywhere, that it is no longer definable by its position in the process of production and that "the means" for the reappropriation of which it fights are no longer definable as means of production in the classical sense, for the very good reason that domination is exerted over people outside enterprises as well as inside them, both in their work and in their lives outside work. There is a central conflict and a central stake, but *there is no longer a central front*. The reappropriation struggle is essentially a struggle to *withdraw and shield from* the (technical, administrative, financial, commercial, urban, etc.) apparatuses spaces which a growing productivity makes potentially available.

These spaces are essentially temporal. The economic apparatus leaves vacant growing swathes of time in the life of each individual and, most importantly, of all individuals taken together. But in order that this time does not appear to be *freed* time – time preserved from all domination – the apparatus does everything in its power to *recolonize* it: that is, to monetize it, commercialize it and transform it into that commodity consumption without either economic rationality or autonomy that is commercial leisure. The reappropriation to which the struggle must be directed is, then, first and foremost, the *social and individual reappropriation of working time* which the economic apparatus is forced to leave vacant for want of being able to make it produce surplus-value – time which will become freed, disposable time only if social individuals are able to make it time for *their* own activities, for their own lives and their own ends.

To force capital and, more generally, the economic apparatus to leave the savings of working time at the free disposal of a society in which economically rational activities can no longer be preponderant; to fight for the expansion of spaces of autonomy in which economic purposes and commodity logic no longer prevail; and to render economic, technical, organizational and urban development favourable to the reappropriation by individuals of time, of their environment, of their model of consumption and their mode of social co-operation: such is, broadly, the perspective which is opening up (or would open up) for a Left which defined itself in terms of the decision to *seize the emancipatory potential of post-industrial civilization*.

It will be objected, no doubt, that all this presupposes the desire and the *capacity* on the part of individuals to reappropriate time. But this is precisely the nature of the cultural change that is currently under way. This development continues to be ignored in France, where the political class, the media and the public services persist in presenting pro- fessional, social and financial success as everyone's main preoccupation and principal "source of identity". The ideal they present is that of the professionally qualified specialist, highly paid, employed full-time and for life – in short, the norm which was that of the wage-based society. French society and public opinion will not have it that for the majority of people that norm no longer represents either a possibility or an aspiration, but merely corresponds to the ruling class's political need to perpetuate the *domination* which the wage relation and the competition to land one of these full-time jobs (which we know, however, are available in insufficient numbers) enable it to exert over people's lives. In other countries, by contrast, attention is being directed to the way social individuals are distancing themselves from their work, to their refusal to identify with it and make it the focus of their lives.

That distancing from work and professional life has been increasing for some fifteen years now, as is shown by periodic surveys and polls, particularly in Scandinavia and Germany and, more recently, in Italy. For only 15 per cent of the German workforce (35 per cent of senior managers) does occupational activity remain more important than non-occupational activities, even though the former is deemed "interesting" by a high majority. The cultural change which is now in progress is termed the "post-materialist revolution" by Ronald Inglehardt, who announced its arrival as early as 1977, and the "new cultural model" by Rainer Zoll and David Yankelovich.[6] Alain Touraine, one of the rare writers in France to swim imperturbably against the current of the dominant ideology, speaks of the appearance "at all levels of social life" of a subject which defines itself not so much by the "capacity to dominate and to transform the world than by the distance it puts between itself and this very capacity, and the apparatuses and discourses that make it operative", for whom "morality ... is defined ... by the will to affirm and to choose oneself".[7]

This choice of autonomy, of "self-realization", is in fact the only response by which the subject can face up to the way society has disintegrated into a multiplicity of specialized, technicized systems, each addressing a partial aspect of social reality and everyday life with no coherence between them. None of these partial systems can perform any integrative role which extends beyond its specific, partial function. Socialization no longer guarantees individuals a *place* in a "social order", no longer ensures a sense of belonging and an "identity". Each person occupies multiple functions, roles and places without being able to identify with any one of them; in consequence, everyone has to construct an identity for him- or herself, to define the right line of conduct for him- or herself. The "quest for identity" is never-ending; adolescence never quite comes to an end: one's home and one's sexual relationships, as well as one's line of work and particular job, are all regarded as temporary, while one "waits" for something which "actually" corresponds to what one is looking for – a fulfilling, socially useful activity which has meaning and prospects, an activity with which one can identify.

Not only does "the rise in youth unemployment, the difficulty of finding even a place as an apprentice, never mind a real training" turn every occupational choice into a random one, with no relation to a sense of vocation or life-project, but

> none of the professional roles offered provides sufficient consistency to justify becoming attached to it.... Adolescent styles of behaviour also become common among adults: experimentation, change, the rejection of a lifelong occupation, the desire to go on learning and extend one's horizon and not get bogged down in routine.... How can the individual find his/her place in society without giving up his/her aspirations and potentialities? ... The ideal pursued is one of continued fulfilment, of openness and availability.... These tendencies also reflect the pressure, imposed by ever more rapid socio-cultural change, to remain mobile and flexible

– and, of course, the way employment has been rendered more precarious.[8]

Individuals have been "forced into autonomy", writes Karl Hörning, as if echoing Sartre's phrase, "condemned to be free".[9] And one can immediately see to what extent, in this situation, the opposition between Left and Right political options will have to be radicalized. From a Left point of view, the freedom (or autonomy) to which individuals are "condemned" does not have to be seen as a curse. As a pure vacant space, undetermined in so far as it is simply *given* by the social system, that freedom must, on the contrary, be *seized* as an opportunity and transformed into an enhanced capacity on the part of subjects to "produce" and realize themselves, individually and collectively, in the form of projects for which they may assume responsibility. In this perspective, the fact of employment becoming precarious is to be interpreted as a loosening of the grip which economically determined work had in the past on the life of the population. It signifies that the economy no longer needs the full and full-time employment of every-one, male and female; and that the object of social policies must be to make the time that has been freed from work effectively available to everyone. The increasingly intermittent, discontinuous, secondary char-acter of the wage relation must be transformed into a new freedom, a new right for each person to interrupt his or her professional activity. And this, of course, demands the guaranteeing of an income which is no longer directly related to the number of hours worked.

On the other hand, any conception which sees autonomy as a calamity, against which the appropriate reaction would be to seek refuge in religious fundamentalism, the commands of an authoritarian order or the constraining exigencies of the economic or technical pursuit of maximum efficiency, will have to be considered a Rightist one. None of these forms of "escape from freedom" will, however, be able to rid complex, modern societies of the "burden" of liberty, nor establish within them stable "identity-bestowing" structures.[10] When, as is currently the case, (national, social, occupational, ethnic or religious) identity is invoked and extolled on all fronts, this proves that it *is in doubt*, that it is no longer self-evident, that it is already lost. Individual being and social being no longer coincide – and can no longer coincide – because this latter is no longer – and no longer can be – a belonging of the individual in his or her entirety to society and community – in work, lifestyle, ethics, milieu and position within the social totality – as was the case in a guild-based society or within the industrial working class, with its culture, solidarities, associations and counter-society. In complex modern society, the differentiation of spheres of activity brings with it a differentiation of the dimensions of existence, and prevents the subject from seeking his or her unity in any of them. The multiplicity of his or her roles introduces a fissure between each of these and him- or herself.

Once this process of differentiation has begun, any attempt to put the clock back, to return to a highly integrative social-communitary *order*, re-establishing the unity of spheres of activity and spheres of life by subordinating them to the rationality of one of those spheres, will have an inevitably totalitarian character: it will block the society's capacity to evolve – its "capacity to act upon itself", as Touraine puts it; or, in Habermas's terminology, the possibility of the lifeworld reacting back on the system. Whether it be fundamentalist, Leninist or fascist, such a social-communitary order will always have a corporatist structure, even if this means dominating the different spheres of activity by placing "elites" recruited and promoted on lines of ideological conformism and political loyalty at the head of each of them.

The differentiation of spheres of activity – and, hence, modernity – will remain unfinished as long as one particular sphere can subordinate others to its logic; as long, for example, as the requirements of capital valorization impose their orientation and imprint on technology, on the definition of needs, on the model of consumption, on the organization of work, and so forth; or as long as the domestication of the "economic subsystem" is based on a reinforced domination of the "administrative-bureaucratic subsystem"; or as long as techno-science colonizes the lifeworld with its apparatuses, and deprives people of the possibility of developing living and lived relations to their environment, to space, to time and to their bodies.

The completion of modernity, and thus the task – in essence still incomplete – by which the Left defines itself consists in putting an end to the situation in which one or more spheres of activity dominate the others, and preventing all the subsystems (apparatuses, in Touraine's terminology) from encroaching on the self-determined spheres of life and activity. It is this *domination* by economic rationality, embodied in capital and its techno-bureaucratic apparatuses, which defines capitalism, not the existence of an economic sphere governed by the logic of profitability and competition. It is the abolition of that domination, not the abolition of capital and the market, which will mark our passing beyond capitalism. Any elimination of the relative autonomy of a sphere of activity reduces the complexity of society and its development potential. The aim can only be to circumscribe, to restrict the field in which each type of rationality is permitted to express itself in an unfettered way. As Alain Touraine continues to point out, this is the objective of the grass-roots social movements.

In the same vein, despite insurmountable methodological differences, Habermas notes that "only the dissident critics of industrial society start from the premise that the lifeworld is equally threatened by commodification *and* bureaucratization" – that is, the dictatorship over needs exerted by capital and the state. "They [the dissident critics] are the only ones to demand that the inner dynamic of subsystems regulated by money and power be broken ... by forms of organization that are closer to the base and self-administered"; it is "not only capitalism but the interventionist state itself" that now has to be "socially contained". This requires "a completely altered relationship between autonomous, self-organized public spheres on the one hand and domains of action regulated by money and administrative power on the other". In other words, the regulatory mechanisms of the state and the economy must themselves be reflectively regulated by a social instance which "could make [them] ... sufficiently sensitive to" a will formed by "radical democratic" procedures, procedures which "would put participants *themselves* in a position to realize concrete possibilities for a better and less threatened life, on *their own* initiative and in accordance with *their own* needs and insights".[11]

Notes

1. Here I pass over the fascist solution, which dresses up an authoritarian capitalist modernization as a social–communitary national-populism.

2. "The New Obscurity", in *The New Conservatism*, Cambridge, MA 1989, pp. 58–9.

3. ibid., p. 60.

4. Cf. Guy Roustang, *L'emploi, un choix de société*, Paris 1987; and Chapter 5 below.

5. Alain Touraine, *The Return of the Actor*, Minneapolis 1988, pp. 41, 49–50.

6. See Ronald Inglehardt, *The Silent Revolution: Changing Values and Political Styles among Western Publics*, Princeton, NJ 1977; Rainer Zoll *et al.*, *Nicht so wie unsere Eltern*, Opladen 1989; David Yankelovich, *New Rules – Searching for Self-Fulfillment in a World Turned Upside Down*, New York 1981.

7. Touraine, *The Return of the Actor*, pp. xxv, 8.

8. Mechtild Oeschsle, in Zoll *et al.*, *Nicht so wie unsere Eltern*, pp. 224–7.

9. Karl H. Hörning *et al.*, *Zeitpioniere. Flexible Arbeitszeiten – neuer Lebensstil*, Frankfurt-am-Main 1990.

10. *Escape from Freedom* is the original title of a work published in 1941 by the Frankfurt School author Erich Fromm, in which the psychological wellsprings of National Socialism are seen as lying in just such an "escape". This same work has been republished more recently as *Fear of Freedom* (London 1960).

11. Habermas, "The New Obscurity", pp. 63–9.

3

Capitalism, Socialism,

Ecology

The text which follows is a commentary on the new long-term programme of the SPD. Written in June 1989 and published in the Party's theoretical journal alongside three other commentaries, it stresses the themes in the new programme which contrast with the traditional orientations of the European Left.[1] Considering the disarray and lack of imagination which predominate in almost all the other great parties of the Left, the SPD's programme seems really innovative in several respects. Its analysis has provided an opportunity to clarify certain notions and themes (particularly the distinctions between capitalism and socialism, and between socially useful and reproductive labour).

The question remains, however, to what extent the revamping of these themes and orientations is likely to renovate the inner life and outward image of an old Left party; or, in other terms, whether the renovators, who emerged from the struggles of the 1960s and 1970s, can really revamp the SPD by opening it up to the new social movements, cultural changes and the European transcendence of the nation-state. Can an old workers' party assimilate new themes and new forms of action, and forge links with new movements, without losing its identity, cohesion, legitimacy and members? Can it reconcile its aspiration to wield power with the broadening of the field of political struggles, a more direct conception of democracy and a corresponding transformation of its own structures?

There seemed to be reason to doubt this after the Berlin congress of November 1989, when the Party programme was pushed into the background in favour of the theme of German unity. The renovation of an old party and the renewal of its ideological themes are never achieved without crises and some initial setbacks. The work of redefining old tasks by taking into account new realities can never be sure of success in the short term. The only sure thing is that the Left has no future if it does not buckle down to that undertaking. What Antje Vollmer said of the Greens goes for the whole of the Left: "We have to perform the feat of responding to the questions both of the nineteenth and of the twenty-first centuries."

1. Because it is the only major party of the Left in Europe's economically most powerful country, the SPD is inevitably a reference point for the rest of the European Left. The problems it confronts are often those which the Left in the other countries will have to face in their turn when their economies reach a comparable level of development. In Central and Eastern Europe, too, the SPD's conception of what socialism can or ought to be in an overdeveloped democratic country is not without influence on the social and political forces which reject the alternative between state-bureaucratic dictatorship and the establishment of a market economy.

The SPD programme seems a pioneering initiative in three fields:

- the ecological restructuring of industrial society;
- the reduction of weekly working hours to thirty spread over five days, to which would also be added the right to a sabbatical year and additional (paid) holidays for the parents of young children and those in need of care – i.e. an average annual working time of around a thousand hours;
- the importance accorded to "feminine values", which are called upon to occupy a place in the lives of men as well as women that is at least equal to that of the "masculine values" of efficiency and productivity. In short, post-capitalist humanism and the end of the productivist society based on labour as a commodity.

Before analysing more closely what these themes imply for a renovated conception of socialism, I shall make a number of preliminary remarks.

2. *Omissions.* The orientations and themes of the programme are most often presented axiomatically and normatively. As a result, some parts of it are strangely abstract. As an outside observer, I am quite pleased that the largest Left party in Europe should address itself to the universal consciousness in this way, rather than to determinate populations with determinate interests; I have a tendency to do the same myself – a fact which, by the way, greatly limits my political tastes and understanding. But as an outside observer, I also doubt whether a programme conceived on these lines is capable both of securing the renewal of a great political party, whose identity has been forged by a long history, and of mobilizing the energies required to put that long-term programme into effect.

At the risk of seeming old-fashioned, I would have liked the programme to explain to me how the past of a long-established workers' party connects with "the world in which we live" and the orientations it proposes for the future. It should have explained where it came from, what has changed since the previous long-term programme (Bad Godesberg, 1959), where the dynamic at work in society – and in international relations – is leading, in what direction that dynamic can be reorientated to avoid the threats it harbours and fulfil the potential for liberation it contains. I should have liked to see something not only on the threat of destruction to the natural foundations of life, but also:

- on the total collapse of entire societies and civilizations in the Americas, in Africa and in southern Asia;
- on the crisis afflicting the notion of work and work itself which, in the great majority of jobs, no longer corresponds in any way to the concept forged by Hegel and Marx (work as the creative objectification of man's domination of matter);
- on the extension of industrialization to new fields of activity;
- on the industrialization of culture;
- on the crisis of the idea of "socialism".

Should the reference to socialism be abandoned (following the precedent of the PCI in abandoning its reference to communism) or does it still have importance, not just in relation to the past but also as a means of specifying the potentialities for emancipation contained in the contradictions of current social and economic processes?

If it is to be retained, socialism will have to be redefined so as to show how its original meaning still has currency for us.

The programme may provide a useful starting point for such an endeavour. In its main themes, it does in fact propose reforms which imply going beyond capitalism to some extent. This is what I shall attempt to demonstrate in what follows.

3. *Socialism.* The socialist movement made it its goal, from the very beginning, to impose limits on economic rationality, as freely expressed in competitive market relations, and to subordinate this to the demands of a higher rationality. The struggle between those who sought to extend and those who sought to restrict the fields in which economic rationality could express itself in an unfettered manner has, from the outset, been the central conflict within capitalist societies. Those societies emerged as a result of the abolition of the (religious, cultural, aesthetic and social) restrictions to which economic rationality was subject in earlier societies.[2] Subsequently, capitalist societies were obliged, under the pressure of objective necessities but also of social struggles, to impose new and increasingly extensive limits on the play of economic rationality (e.g. the outlawing of slavery, of child labour, of the sale of wives; limiting the

working day; making Sunday a rest day; the minimum wage; health insurance; etc.).

From the socialist point of view, these limitations should impose a framework and a set of operating conditions on economic rationality which would subordinate it, in the end, to the aims of a society in which men and women would no longer be in any way in thrall to need or servitude. By contrast, in a capitalist perspective, it is society which has to be subordinated to the valorization of capital, the economic rationality of which is most surely guaranteed by the unfettered play of market laws.

This central conflict has lost nothing of its acuteness and significance, though the social actors have changed considerably over the last hundred and sixty years.

Socialism may, therefore, be understood as the positive response to the disintegration of social bonds ensuing from the commodity and competitive relations characteristic of capitalism. That response is delivered chiefly by the dependent workers, or in their name. Where market and competitive relations (which also have a positive dimension) have never developed, "socialism", for want of a social base, can only ever be an educative dictatorship with economic modernization as its goal. Such a dictatorship inevitably turns the socialism to which it pays lip service into its opposite: it subordinates society to the requirements of an economic apparatus that has yet to be constructed.

What is at stake in the conflict between capitalism and socialism is not economic rationality as such, but the extent of the sphere in which economic rationality may exert its effects. An action is termed economically rational in so far as it tends to maximize the efficiency with which the factors of production are employed. Efficiency in the economic sense is measured by the profit realized per quantum of living or dead labour (circulating or fixed capital) employed. Whatever the property relations, there is no other economically rational way of managing an enterprise than the capitalist way. This is an obvious point which everyone now accepts. However, as to the extent to which the requirements of economic rationality will prevail over other types of rationality within the enterprise and the national economy, the capitalist and socialist responses will differ.

A society remains capitalist so long as the relations shaped by economic rationality and functional to the valorization of capital are preponderant and mould the lives and activities of individuals, their scale of values and culture. A society becomes socialist when the social relations shaped by the economic rationality of capital come to occupy only a subordinate place in relation to non-quantifiable values and goals, and, in consequence, in the life of society and in each person's life, economically rational work is merely one activity among others of equal importance.

4. *Economic policy.* The conception I have just summarized is exemplified in certain passages of the programme, which imposes new and sometimes radical limitations on economic rationality. For example, one finds the following formulations in the chapter devoted to "economic democracy": "Societal goals are to take precedence over the demands of the valorization of private capital"; "the market must not determine the directions in which society develops. It must not decide in society's stead what technologies and what sectors of activity are to be developed"; "the state lays down the framework and conditions for economic development" and "must promote desirable developments"; "state and local plans lay down in advance objectives and orientations which enterprises must take into account in their decisions"; the "setting of the political framework and the co-ordination of enterprise and state plans" is to "make clear the general interest", and must "be worked out with the participation of economic and social commissions". French-style planning, practically abandoned in the 1970s, seems called upon here to rise from the grave.

Given the central importance accorded to the reduction of working hours in the programme, one might have expected that the chapter on economic policy would have indicated, if only briefly, that the reduction of working hours is not just an isolated measure, but an overall policy – and one that also implies a policy on time, co-ordination of the plans of enterprises and administrative bodies, and the participation of the trade unions from the preparatory phase onwards. It might also have been pointed out that the cost of reducing working hours cannot simply be borne by each enterprise but demands public financing which neither causes price distortion nor blocks competition.[3] The lapidary statement "we shall work out models of financing" sounds almost comical: why did the SPD not set about this long ago?

Regarding the orientation and goals which the limitation of economic rationality is to subserve, the programme lays down two essential projects: ecological restructuring and the extension of the spheres of activity and life that are to be freed from economic constraints.

5. *Ecological restructuring.* The chapter devoted to ecological restructuring (or "modernization") enumerates convincingly the sectors most urgently in need of transformation: "The ecological restructuring of our economy, from product design [products will have to be 'durable' and

'easy to repair'] to the consumption and recycling of materials, ... concerns all forms of production and transformation of energy", and demands "the ecological restructuring of the chemical industry, transport and agriculture". This latter is dealt with extensively and in detail.

The ecological reshaping of the industrial system relates particularly to heavy and capital-intensive industries. The chemical industry, for example, will have to undergo a substantial fall in its sales as a result of the move towards an agriculture "which respects natural balances". This latter will spend only a fraction of what was spent by chemical agriculture on fertilizers and pest control. The development of urban and suburban public transport, the priority granted to rail over road in the carrying of goods and passengers, speed limits, and the use of durable means of transport that are easy to repair and "ecologically sound" will lead to a fall in automobile production. The development of public transport will not offer substitute outlets to industry on the same scale. Industry will neither be able, nor will it be required, to grow. "Those activities must grow which secure the basic elements of life and improve its quality ... [which] promote self-determination and autonomous creative activities. Those activities which threaten the natural foundations of life must diminish and disappear."

"Technical innovation must not only serve ecological restructuring and rationalization", it must also "raise the productivity of labour, make possible shorter working hours", and "free us from alienated labour". In short, the economic criteria of maximum productivity and profitability are subordinated to socio-ecological criteria.

Now, the economic imperative of productivity is totally different from the ecological imperative of resource conservation. Ecological rationality consists in satisfying material needs in the best way possible with as small a quantity as possible of goods with a high use-value and durability, and thus doing so with a minimum of work, capital and natural resources. The quest for maximum economic productivity, by contrast, consists in selling at as high a profit as possible the greatest possible quantity of goods produced with the maximum of efficiency, all of which demands a maximization of consumption and needs. Only by such a maximization is it possible to obtain a return on growing quantities of capital. As a consequence, the pursuit of maximum productivity at the enterprise level leads to increasing waste in the economy as a whole. But what appears, from the ecological point of view, as a waste and destruction of resources is perceived from the economic point of view as a source of growth: competition between enterprises speeds up innovation, and the volume of sales and velocity of capital circulation increase as a result of obsolescence and the more rapid renewal of products. And what, from the ecological point of view, seems a saving (product durability, prevention of illness and accidents, lower energy and resource consumption) reduces the production of economically measurable wealth in the form of GNP, and appears on the macro-economic level as a source of loss.

The chapter devoted to "economic democracy" recognizes this contradiction between ecological and economic rationality ("an economy becomes ecologically and socially responsible only when democratic decisions take precedence over the pursuit of profit and economic power"), but the chapter devoted to ecological restructuring attempts to argue that these two rationalities are one:

> In the long term, what is ecologically unreasonable cannot be economically rational.... Ecological necessities have to become the basic principles of economic activity. If we set about ecological modernization in time, we shall improve our chances of conquering tomorrow's markets and improve the competitiveness of our economy.

This last assertion alone has some truth in it. Those who are first to develop the economic production of solar energy, hydrogen motors and the storage of hydrogen, methods of biological pest control, and so on, may hope to win new outlets and obtain a return on substantial quantities of capital. But it would be an illusion to believe – and paradoxical to hope – that ecological rationalization can compensate for the decline and conversion of the classical industries by employing in an "environmental economy" the labour and capital that are saved elsewhere. For a great many enterprises, ecological conversion can be an engine of growth during the transitional period, but this cannot be the long-term goal from the macro-economic point of view. Industry and the economy as a whole cannot take the view that, thanks to ecological modernization, they will end up in a better condition; they must simply accept that without ecological modernization they will soon be in a much worse one. This is a policy for which there is no alternative, and one which must not be presented as an option motivated by the economic opportunities it affords. It has to be recognized that this policy runs counter to economic interests (the interests of capital) by emphasizing that it is quite simply impossible to continue as in the past, and that inactivity and indecision would have catastrophic consequences which would also make their impact on the economy.

Ecological rationalization can be summed up in the slogan "less but better". Its aim is a society in which we live better while working and consuming less. Ecological modernization requires that investment no longer serve the growth of the economy but its contraction – that is to say, it requires the sphere governed by economic rationality in the modern sense to shrink. There can be no ecological modernization without restricting the dynamic of capitalist accumulation and reducing consumption by self-imposed restraint. The exigencies of ecological modernization coincide with those of a transformed North–South relationship, and with the original aims of socialism.

The change in culture which this presupposes is precisely the one which is outlined in Chapter IV of the programme.

6. *Cultural change.* "As the amount that has to be spent on basic needs diminishes, greater scope is created for education, culture, social interaction and meaningful leisure. This is why we shall promote growth in these areas." The expansion in question here is obviously not of an economic nature; it has nothing to do with the development of the culture industry, the leisure or personal services industries which advocates of "tertiarization" expect to deliver a great number of jobs. There is a fundamental difference between economic activities and cultural activities. Economic rationality is a resolutely instrumental rationality: the means deployed are distinct from the objectives pursued, and these latter are themselves means of valorizing capital. But this kind of utilitarian calculation is not applicable in cases where the objective of the activity is realized *in* (and not *by means of*) that activity itself, as is the situation in all caring activities in which the care taken of people, animals or objects, the care with which the various arts and faculties are cultivated, is of use for nothing *else*.

This is why it is erroneous to refer to all activities as "work", in order then to conclude that "there is no shortage of work in our society". What is, in fact, in short supply is work for economic ends and purposes, work that can be socialized and monetized; by contrast, there is no lack of tasks which are not economically rational and rationalizable and which, for that reason, have never been granted consideration or developed as they deserve. These distinctions are already to be found in the work of Adam Smith, who characterized as unproductive – that is, lying outside economic rationality – service [i.e. labour] "which produces nothing for which an equal quantity of service can afterwards be procured". "Unproductive labourers, and those who do not labour at all," he added, "are all maintained by revenue" – that is, by an income paid out of surplus-value.

The many "jobs left undone" and the many "needs left untended" are neglected and unfinished precisely because they are not subject to economic criteria and cannot be evaluated in economic terms. As a consequence, they must be taken care of either by "services financed out of public funds" (i.e. by being paid out of surplus-value) or by people themselves, individually or in mutual aid groups. It is absurd to desire, as the programme does, "to accord the same value to all forms of socially necessary work", since not all activities in which people engage have the same value or conform to the same type of rationality, and some of them are not – and must not be – motivated by social necessity. We do not bring children into the world out of social necessity, nor do we raise them for that reason. The same applies to maintaining our houses and our bodies, and this indeed is why we do not accord society the right to prescribe, supervise or evaluate all these activities.

The social utilitarianism of the following statement is particularly unacceptable: "The state and society are dependent on the services rendered by family life-communities. *For this reason* [emphasis added], they have a right to expect to be protected and encouraged." This utilitarian approach is incompatible with a project which seeks to base itself on each person's right to determine the conduct of his or her life for him- or herself, and find fulfilment as an individual. Who ever entered a life-community *because* "the state and society" were "dependent" on their so doing? To be correct, the formulation would have to be reversed: "Life-communities are indispensable to the fulfilment of the person. *For that reason*, the state and society must protect and encourage them in the name of the inalienable rights of the person."

A social project of the Left should start out from the fact that there are activities which deserve to be done on their own account – activities on which the meaning and quality of life, and individual development and sovereignty, depend, but to which, as a result of the dominance of economic rationality, time and social recognition have never been granted. The point, then, is to act so that social time becomes available for these activities. And this will actually serve to reinforce the demand that paid and unpaid activities be fairly divided up between men and women.

I find it particularly cheering that, for the first time (so far as I am aware) in history, the programme of a major political party stresses the importance of "feminine values" such as "sensitivity" and "imagination", "love and conviviality, dreaming and thinking". "Men, too, are becoming aware that the supposedly manly subordination of feeling and imagination to rationality and efficiency impoverishes them and even makes them ill. For society to become human, it has to cease to be manly." This could be Herbert Marcuse, writing in 1969:

> The future demands of us, women and men, many qualities which were long regarded as feminine. . . . The education of young people must prepare them for this. It must assist in overcoming the division of the world into masculine and feminine worlds.
>
> Like the ability to reason, sensitivity too requires education.

Everyone, male and female, must have the opportunity to engage in activities which concern our locality or environment, and trade union or political life, ... to be creative, to make music, write or engage in the fine arts, to do sport or busy ourselves in the garden or workshop. Local politics and the education system must see to it that the conditions for pursuing these activities are improved.

We must introduce the six-hour day within the context of a five-day week in order that women and men can better combine their occupational activity, domestic and family tasks and voluntary and cultural activities.

Furthermore, the programme makes provision for "paid parental leave and paid leave to tend the sick". These, indeed, are measures which would put an end to the dominance of economic values, and open up the way to a socialist society.

The influence of the women's movement seems to have borne fruit here. As for the politico-cultural subjects who might put these orientations into practice, the programme offers the following observations, with which I entirely concur:

Civic initiatives and social movements modify the conception of the world and are, at the same time, an expression of changed consciousness. They ensure that important topics are debated; they enliven our democracy by creating new forms of political will-formation and they generally enrich our political culture. They can and, indeed, must pose ever renewed challenges to the political parties, but they can never replace them.

The political culture grows stale without the tension between future projects and the present reality. Future projects have a bearing only if millions of conscious citizens, male and female, see their hopes reflected in them. Only where people ... can express their convictions and fears in the political sphere ... can politics free itself from being a mere ratification of objective exigencies and carry through essential reforms.

These latter must be carried forward by an

alliance of the old and new social movements. Collaboration with the trade unions remains the central axis of this alliance. But it must also include all those who, by their daily experience or their involvement in the new social movements, have become convinced of the need for fundamental reforms.

Mi va bene così.

Notes

1. *Neue Gesellschaft/Frankfurter Hefte* (ed. Peter Glotz), August 1989.
2. For more details, see A. Gorz, *Critique of Economic Reason*, London 1989, Part II, chapters 1 and 2.
3. These points are developed in Chapters 8 and 9 below.

4

Redefining Socialism*

1. The question is not whether socialism "in itself" (whatever that might be) has a future, but whether, or in what form, conflicts, contradictions, needs and aspirations keep developing which require capitalism to be overcome and contain at least the seeds of non-capitalist concepts. What socialism can or should be will emerge from the way in which the developing conflicts and contradictions are experienced and interpreted. Socialism will never be achieved as the outcome of a "scientific" project; it will always be dependent on interpretations reflecting the self-understanding, subjectivity, lived cultural and political relationships of the actors.

The concept of "scientific socialism" has lost all meaning. Within so-called "real socialism", the supposed scientificity of its precepts had the practical function of dismissing people's needs, desires and protests as "unscientific" and "subjective", and subordinating them to the systemic imperatives of the industrial apparatus which was to be established. "Real socialist" planning conceived of society as a centrally directed industrial machinery, and required individuals to conform to that machinery's demands. Their life was to be completely rationalized – that is, organized functionally by the bureaucratic-industrial mega-machine. Resistance to this functionalization, which in many respects resembled militarization, was condemned as petty-bourgeois or philistine individualism.

To the extent that it understood itself as a *system* which, in the name of the scientificity of its total rationalization, cut itself off from any

---

Translator's note: A version of this article first appeared in *Neue Gesellschaft/Frankfurter Hefte* 6, 1990.

moorings in the lifeworld, and blocked individuals' aspirations to emancipation and autonomy, socialism is dead. But socialism will continue to exist or revive again as a movement and historical horizon if, in keeping with its original meaning, it understands itself as striving to carry through the emancipation of individuals begun by the bourgeois revolution – that is, to realize that emancipation also in areas in which, under capitalism, individuals remain subordinated to systemic constraints, relations of dominance and alienation.

2. Consequently, socialism can be understood only in relation to capitalism, of which it is the positive negation.[1] It has its origin in the ambiguity and incompleteness of capitalist modernization, in the intolerable effects of the free market economy. Everywhere it was introduced, the latter brought not only elements of radical emancipation but also new forms of exploitation and alienation. For the first time in history, individuals were freed from the despotism of the state or of princes, or from hierarchical dependency, and were granted the right to pursue their own material interests. As is well known, this right which was conceded to them unleashed the struggle "of each against all" in free markets. Unrestricted competition forced every business to use the factors of production as efficiently as possible – that is, to seek to maximize productivity, innovation, profit and investment.

Economic rationality was freed by the logic of the market from the religious, ethical, normative social precepts which, in earlier societies, had restricted its scope. Capitalism was and is the only form of society which makes competition, with the aim of maximizing productivity and profit, its first commandment, unremittingly striving to enrol society, education, labour, individual and collective consumption into the service of the greatest possible valorization of capital and, consequently, to extend the domination of economic rationality, which expresses itself unchecked in the logic of the market, to all areas of life and work.

The socialist movement grew out of the struggle carried on by individuals united in solidarity to impose new social restrictions, based on ethical demands, on the sphere in which economic rationality can operate. Only such restrictions can guarantee the workers' personal integrity and their right individually and collectively to self-determine how they live their lives. The import and purpose of the socialist movement has been – and still is – the emancipation of individuals in fields where the logic of market, competition and profit functions to prevent individuals from achieving autonomy and fulfilment.

3. The history of capitalism contradicts the frequently heard assertion that there is no third way between the market economy and the defunct "real socialist" central state planning. It is true, however, that industrialized economic systems are and will remain capitalist, as long as the logic of the greatest possible return on the largest possible quantities of (fixed and circulating) capital determines working conditions, investment decisions, consumption and, consequently, the way of life, education and values. But it is obvious that even capitalist economic systems absolutely require the planning of both private and public investments (e.g. in the areas of research, development, education, training, infrastructure, energy and health policies) and the regulation and correction of the markets' workings through public interventions, subsidies and taxes on production or consumption. Equally, they quite obviously need to keep the logic of the market and unrestrained competition within limits laid down by social laws and institutions.

The fact that these limitations on the scope of economic rationality expressed through market laws are repeatedly attacked and denounced by the advocates of the free market economy demonstrates how central the conflict between, on the one hand, the economic rationality embodied in the logic of capital and, on the other, non-economic, individual and societal, needs and demands remains. The "welfare" state is a more or less humanized capitalism, not a democratic socialism. Its social laws were stuck on top of capitalism – or tacked on, as it were. What results from this process is not socialism, since social-state regulations create no sociability, no lived solidarity. They merely compensate for the decay, brought about by market and commodity relations, of grass-roots communities and of social cohesion anchored in the lifeworld, and thereby accelerate both that decay and an ever greater spread of commodity and cash relationships. The welfare state becomes the guardian of the general interest against the "every man for himself" of market society, and also promotes the latter, in that it takes over and administers the general interest as an instance separated from civil society.

It is possible to talk of socialism only when the bureaucratic-industrial system, its power apparatuses and technical constraints, are limited and restructured in such a way that the whole sphere of economically rational activities is enrolled in the service of forms of co-operation and exchange determined by social individuals themselves, and so retains only a subordinate significance.

4. Socialism as horizon of meaning, as emancipatory utopia, must not be conceived of as a different economic and social *system*. Quite the

contrary: it is the conscious practical project of abolishing everything that makes society a system, a megamachine, together with the simultaneous expansion of autonomous self-regulated forms of sociability, which make possible "the free development of individuality".

In this respect there is no sharp distinction between the utopian contents of socialism and communism. For us *today* they are distinct, because communism looks forward to the complete removal of commodity relations, of wage-labour and the social division of labour, of state administration and control – as if "system" could be completely transferred to "lifeworld", and even complex industrial societies could be self-governing like a kibbutz, or regress to self-sufficient communes. Whereas socialism, in my opinion, does not aim to abolish the economic and administrative systems, but only to limit and bind them into the lifeworld, so that a synergy with self-determined social and individual forms of living results.

For socialists it is a question, to an increasing extent, of organizing society and sociability as spaces for individual emancipation and development, and of demonstrating the concrete possibility of such a reappropriation and self-organization of social life in their political, trade-union and cultural practice. Only through such solidaristic association and voluntary co-operation can individuals free themselves from their subordination to the uncontrolled logic of capital and market forces to become actors in the creation of a new society. To fight for socialism means concretely to claim the right of individuals to freedom, equality, physical integrity and self-determination, by acting so that the social conditions which conflict with this right are remodelled. Interestingly, Rainer Land's noteworthy *Umbaupapier* (Reconstruction Paper) also tends in this same direction:

> For me, socialism is a society which evolves in such a way as to create growing spaces for the development of individuals in the fields of material civilization, work, the environment and consumption. . . . A style of life and consumption which is rich but makes small demands on natural resources, which allows a great many varied subcultures to develop and expands the scope for individual autonomy – these are the emerging values of a new conception of rationality. It will become a reality when all economic decision-makers develop their strategies and determine their decisions on the basis of the felt needs and lived interests of individuals themselves in their democratic organizations, associations and initiatives.[2]

5. Overcoming capitalism will come to be regarded as an urgent task when capitalism's systemic imperatives are seen as incompatible with the

preservation of life – as threatening not only its foundations, but also the possibility of conferring meaning upon it.

It no longer makes sense to expect the pressure of needs engendered by work to lead to a socialist transformation of society, or for such a transformation to be effected by the working class alone. The class antagonism between labour and capital still exists, but it now has superimposed upon it antagonisms which are not of the order of workplace struggles and relations of exploitation, and thus are not covered by traditional class analysis.

It is not through identification with their work and their work role that modern wage-earners feel themselves justified in making demands for power which have the potential to change society. It is as citizens, residents, parents, teachers, students or as unemployed; it is their experience outside work that leads them to call capitalism into question. The radical critique of capitalism is not so much the result of the work experience itself as of the critical distance the workers take in respect of their work role; it is a result of the surplus individual capacities and social competencies which find no possibility of development within the work role; of the antagonism between *possible* quality of life, self-realization and autonomy on the one hand and the compulsion to maximize productivity and profit on the other. The competitive struggle between sectors of capital leads in every country to a reduction of social services, the reintroduction of night and weekend working, lack of job security, the marginalization of increasing sections of the population, the deterioration of the environment and quality of life – in short, *to the surrender of the essential, so that the inessential can be produced as profitably and cheaply as possible.*

Even more than their labour-power, the technical apparatuses of capital expropriate individuals' lived relationships and their senses. It is only eco-socialist modernization, not the ecological restructuring of industrial society, that can offer solutions, in this respect, which are neither technocratic nor authoritarian. A policy of free choice of working hours, expanded possibilities of self-determined activity and democratization of economic decision-making are the only paths which lead in freedom to a more frugal, ecologically sustainable consumer model based on self-restraint.

The other path, that of an ecological modernization of capitalism, involves just as many dangers as the destruction of the natural bases of life – which it threatens to continue in other ways. The reproduction of the "natural" bases of life can itself be industrialized and developed into a profitable eco-business, obeying the same imperatives of profitability as other consumer goods industries: in other words, satisfying basic needs not as well and as rationally as possible, but with the largest possible flow of profitable commodities. An ecological techno-fascism would also be capable of reproducing the bases of life, by artificially replacing natural cycles, turning nature into business, as it were, and so industrializing the reproduction of life, even of human life, commodifying foetuses and organs and instrumentalizing genetic stock, including that of humans, in accordance with the demands of productivity and profit maximization. The trend is obvious: the unleashing of economic rationality, its offensive against ethical objections which attempt to set limits to it, is already under way.

"The redefinition of socialism", writes the Viennese historian Siegi Mattl,

> can no longer proceed by the familiar pathways because capital is in the process of abrogating the 'social contract,' of which bourgeois society, in Europe at least, has until now been so proud. For the first time in history, socialism really faces the prospect of having to embody everything that constitutes humanity – solidarity, rebellion, the capacity for social and cultural creation and self-determination. These are not, however, by-products of capitalist development, but products of opposition and subversion.... What is at stake here is the revolutionary project in which people are something other than – more than – functionaries of a social machine; at stake is autonomy, the possibility that human beings may enter into truly free associations in which the domination of others – whether it take the form of the Ten Commandments, state power or share ownership – is no longer possible. If it is to survive, socialism will have to remember its origins of a hundred years ago. Those origins lay, to a greater extent than its present heirs are willing to admit, in an alliance of subversions.[3]

Translated by Martin Chalmers and Chris Turner

Notes

1. What Oskar Negt has written with reference to China may be considered valid for all "real socialist" systems: "So long as central problems of the democratic constitution of a society are not solved, the political moment of the bourgeois revolution remain the central theme' *Modernisierung im Zeichen des Drachen*, Frankfurt-am-Main 1988.

2. Rainer Land and Michael Brie, *Das Umbaupapier,* Berlin 1990. This book is the draft programme of radical-democratic reforms elaborated in the late 1980s by a group of oppositional East German Marxists.

3. Siegi Mattl, "Was bleibt vom Sozialismus?", in *Mit wem zieht die neue Zeit?*, Sommerwerkstatt Steyr 88 (Vienna n.d.).

5

The New Servants[1]

Since the beginning of the modern era, one question has constantly faced Western societies: to what extent is economic rationality compatible with that minimum of social cohesion a society needs if it is to survive? The same question confronts us today, in new forms and with even greater urgency and intensity.

There is a striking contrast between the realities which bring this question home to us and the soothing tones of the dominant ideology. I shall therefore begin by recalling a number of basic facts.

In the capitalist countries of Europe, taken as a whole, three to four times more wealth is produced today than thirty-five years ago. But it does not take three times more hours of work to achieve this more-than-tripled level of production. It requires a much lower quantity.

In the Federal Republic of Germany, the total annual volume of work has decreased by 30 per cent since 1955. In France, it decreased by 15 per cent in thirty years, and by 10 per cent in the space of six years. The consequences of these gains in productivity are summarized as follows by Jacques Delors. In 1946, a twenty-year-old wage-earner could expect to spend a third of his or her waking life at work; by 1975, the figure was a quarter; today, it is less than a fifth. And even then, this figure does not take account of the productivity gains that will be achieved in the future, and holds only for workers employed full-time over the whole year. From this point on, added Delors, French people aged over fifteen will spend less time at work than they do watching television.

The meaning of these figures – a meaning which our civilization, press and political representatives prefer not to confront – is that we are no longer living in a society of producers, in a work-based civilization. Work is no longer the main social cement, the principal factor of socialization, nor each person's main occupation, their chief source of wealth and well-being, the meaning and focus of our lives. We are leaving the work-based society behind, but we are exiting backwards from it and walking backwards into a civilization of free time, incapable of visualizing and desiring that civilization, and thus incapable of *civilizing* the free time which is coming our way; incapable of creating a culture of free time and a culture of chosen activities to take over from and complement the technicist and professional cultures which currently hold centre stage. Everything we do remains dominated by the concern for efficiency, productivity and optimum performance, and hence by the concern to obtain the best possible outcome with the minimum of work in the minimum of time. And we seem intent upon ignoring the fact that the chief consequence of our drive towards efficiency and economic rationalization is that it frees us from work, frees up our time, releases us from the rule of economic rationality itself – an outcome which economic rationality is incapable either of evaluating or of endowing with meaning.

This inability of our societies to establish a civilization based on free time leads to a completely absurd and scandalously unjust distribution of work, disposable time and wealth. All eyes are on the new careers opened up by the micro-electronic revolution and the fundamental transformations it is bringing about in the nature of industrial work and, particularly, in the condition of the workers. We are told that repetitive and mindless tasks are tending to disappear from industry, that industrial work is steadily becoming absorbing, responsible work, organized by the workers themselves and varied in its nature, requiring self-starting individuals with initiative and communications skills who are able to acquire and master a wide variety of intellectual and manual disciplines. A new class of craft workers, we are told, is taking over from the old working class and realizing the old dream of the producers holding power at the site of production and organizing their own work there, answerable to no one.

And if you ask what proportion of employees enjoy such new conditions, you are told that today it is only 5 to 10 per cent of workers in industry, but tomorrow it will be 25 per cent, or even 40 to 50 per cent in the metalworking industries.

This is all very well. But what will become of the 75 per cent of workers in industry and the 50 or 60 per cent of workers in the metalworking industries who will not attain the enviable condition just described? And what will become of those, both male and female, who do not work in industry? Isn't their number growing? Isn't industry laying off labour? Isn't it, in the medium and long term, reducing its workforce? Hasn't the proportion of the active population working in industry fallen from around 40 per cent twenty years ago to around 30 per cent today, and isn't it forecast that it will be less than 20 per cent in ten years or so? What is to become, then, of this labour which industry ... "releases", if one may put it that way, in order to leave it with just those precious multiskilled professionals whose allegiance it gains by offering them a privileged income and status?

We know the answers to these questions, but we prefer not to face up to their disturbing, dismaying import. In actual fact, for almost half of the active population, the ideology of work is a bad joke and identification with work an impossibility, since the economic system has no need – or no regular need – of their capacities. The reality disguised by extolling "human resources" or the work of the new skilled industrial personnel is that stable, full-time, year-round employment throughout an entire lifetime is becoming the privilege of a minority, and that for almost half of the active population, work no longer takes the form of an occupation which integrates them into a productive community and defines their place in society.

The situation in France is in no way exceptional in this regard. France, in effect, not only has two and a half million unemployed, but also three million employed people in jobs that are termed "outside the norm" or atypical: temporary, casual, part-time or illusorily "independent" jobs. More than two-thirds of the new jobs created in France are in this category, and the situation is no different in the Federal Republic: half of the new jobs created there are part-time or casual; a third of the total workforce have temporary or part-time jobs, with corresponding wages. And when the statistics show a fall in the jobless total, one should not conclude that the economy once again needs a greater volume of work. To reduce the unemployment rate, one can also increase the proportion of part-time and part-waged jobs to the detriment of full-time work. This is what has been happening in the Federal Republic over the last few years.

The situation is even more characteristic in the United States and Great Britain, where the development to which we are referring began some years earlier. In these two countries, the unemployed and those employed part-time and on a casual basis together represent more than 45 per cent of the active population. In Great Britain, 50 per cent of women and 25 per cent of men – that is to say, 36 per cent of the total labour force – are in jobs "outside the norm". Ninety per cent of the jobs created over a five-year period in Great Britain were casual and/or part-time. In the United States, 60 per cent of the jobs created during the 1980s had wages below the poverty level; the typical income of an American family in which the husband is under twenty-five is 43 per cent lower today than it was in 1973.

Hence between 35 and 50 per cent of the active British, French,

German and American populations live on the margins of our so-called work-based civilization, on the fringes of its scale of values, its ethic of productivity and merit. The social system is splitting in two, and giving rise to what is currently termed a "dual" or "two-speed" society. The effect of this is a very rapid disintegration of the social fabric. At the top, there is frantic competition to land one of those rare stable jobs offering access to a career ladder. This is what a perfectly repulsive advertising slogan refers to as the "will to win at any cost". Society is presented in terms of combat sports, social relations are presented in terms of all-out struggle; military vocabulary and warlike images abound. Those, both male and female, who are neither winners nor earners find themselves ejected on to the margins of a society which has nothing to offer them and with which they have few reasons to identify. The violence of that society provokes counter-violence, disaffection, and aggressively regressive or reactionary nostalgia.

This disintegration of a fragmented society brings us back to a fundamental problem: what form must a society take in which full-time work on the part of all its citizens is no longer either necessary or economically useful? What priorities other than economic ones must it accord itself? How must it proceed so that productivity gains and savings in working time redound to everyone's advantage? How can it best redistribute all the socially useful work in such a way that everyone may work – but work less and better – while receiving their share of the socially produced wealth?

The prevailing tendency is to brush aside such questions and pose the problem the other way round – to ask: how can we proceed so that, in spite of productivity gains, the economy still consumes as much work as it did in the past? How are we to proceed so that new paid activities come to take the place of the time which is set free, in overall terms, by productivity gains? To what new fields of activity can commodity exchange be extended so as somehow to replace other jobs lost elsewhere in industry and industrialized services?

You know the answer to these questions, an answer for which the United States and Japan have shown the way: the only field in which it is possible, *within a liberal economy*, to create a large number of jobs for the future is that of personal services. There might be no limits to the development of employment if it were possible to transform into acts of paid service those activities which people have hitherto performed for themselves. Economists speak in this connection of "new employment-richer growth", of "tertiarization" of the economy, and of the development of a "service society" which will take over from "industrial society".

But we shall see that this way of seeking to rescue the wage-earning society raises problems and presents contradictions which deserve a place in the forefront of public debate and political thinking. What is the content, what is the meaning, of the majority of the activities currently being talked of for conversion into professionalized and monetized services? It is easy to show that the professionalization of these services no longer obeys the same logic as the economic development of the past.

In the past, economic growth did, in effect, have "productive substitution" as its engine: tasks which people had for centuries performed in their domestic sphere were progressively transferred to industry and service industries which possessed machines more efficient than those to which a household had access. Industrial production and industrialized services thus replaced "own-use" production within the home, and supplanted individuals' provision for themselves. No one spins their own wool any longer, or weaves their cloth, makes their clothes, bakes their bread, makes their jams, builds their house, and so forth, since all these activities, which people still frequently performed for themselves two or three generations ago, are carried on more quickly, and often better, by industries employing wage-labourers. And because industrialization allows us to do a host of things more quickly and often better with less work, everyone can, in the end, buy more goods and services with the wages for one hour of their work than they would be able to produce by and for themselves in the space of one hour. In other words, industrialization has saved working time for everyone, throughout society, and the working time saved has been re-employed to a large extent *within the economy* to produce extra wealth which only industrialization enables us to conceive and create.

But the question the present course of development raises is precisely this: is it still possible to re-employ *within the economy* the working time saved thanks to the micro-electronic revolution? Do the new jobs created in personal services provide more efficiently – that is to say, *better and more quickly* – the services which people previously performed for themselves? If you examine the great majority of the jobs created in the United States over the last ten years or so, you can see that this is not the case at all. These jobs, which have made it possible to reduce the unemployment rate, do not correspond to what we referred to a moment ago as the "productive substitution" of waged work for individuals' own production for themselves. The function of these jobs, in most cases, is, rather, the following: the two, three or four hours you spent up to now mowing your lawn, walking your dog, doing your shopping, buying your newspaper, doing the housework or taking care of your children are transferred to one or more service-providers who take over these activities in exchange for payment. They do nothing which you could not do just as well yourself. They simply free three or four hours of your time by allowing you to buy three or four hours of theirs. Economists call this kind of transfer "equivalent substitution", and even Adam Smith, in his day, stressed that such a transfer is economically "unproductive". To buy someone else's time to increase your own leisure or comfort is merely to purchase the work of a servant. The majority of the jobs created in the United States are servants' jobs, as indeed are a large proportion of those which, in Japan, explain the low rate of unemployment there. But who is interested in purchasing, and who can afford to purchase, the services of the new servants? This is the embarrassing question which those – including trade unionists – who regard job-creation as an end in itself do not ask.

Suppose, for a moment, that the new servants are in the same position as you – that is to say, for one hour of their work you have to pay them as much as you earn in one hour of yours. From an economic point of view, it would then be more rational for you to work one hour less yourself and look after your own domestic tasks, either individually or within a service-exchange co-operative formed with your neighbours. You will perhaps object that your decision is not entirely determined by the economic aspect: even if one hour's servant work costs you as much as you earn yourself in an hour, you are prepared to pay that price to be rid of all kinds of chores. But if this is the case, *you are claiming the privilege of unloading your chores on to someone else*; you are implicitly asserting that there must be people prepared to take on your chores, *people who are fit only to do what you find boring or repugnant* – in short, people whose vocation is to serve. In a word, inferiors. But why might there be such people? In what social conditions are people prepared to take on other people's chores on a professional basis, as it were, in addition to their own chores? And where do you get the extra purchasing power which enables you to buy increasing quantities of personal services from a growing host of service-providers?

Most economists, and even a number of trade unionists, give the following reply: automation brings down the relative prices of a great many products. This fall in prices increases purchasing power and enables people to afford household services. The reasoning is impeccable, but an essential aspect of the question is left out of account: *where does the fall in relative prices due to automation come from?* The answer is that it comes from *automated enterprises having reduced their "payroll", from their having reduced the volume of wages they distribute*. They have reduced the "payroll" *by reducing their workforce*. The people who now have additional purchasing power by virtue of the fall in prices are obviously not those who have lost their old jobs. Only those who have kept their permanent jobs, which are often relatively well-paid ones with a higher status, have additional purchasing power. Only they can afford the new commodity services provided by the sector in which millions of wage-earners are now supposed to find jobs.

This is the true meaning of the development of personal services. These services are developing, and are likely to create a large number of jobs, because in most cases those who perform an hour of domestic labour in your stead earn much less than you can earn in an hour of *your* work. Personal services are developing as a result of the pauperization of a growing mass of people, a pauperization found both in Western Europe and in North America. Social and economic inequality between those who provide personal services and those who purchase them has become the engine of employment growth. This is based on a dualization of society, on a kind of South-Africanization, as though the colonial model were finding a foothold in the metropolitan heartlands.[2]

Hence we see conditions which prevailed a hundred and fifty years ago, at the outset of the industrial era – a time when the level of consumption was ten times lower than it is today, and there was neither universal suffrage nor compulsory schooling – becoming re-established in the post-industrial age. At that period, too, at the height of the unfettered market economy, one-sixth of the population was reduced to seeking employment as domestic servants in the houses of the rich, and a quarter got by as best they could from occasional work. But in the last century that quarter and that sixth were made up of illiterate rustics and ruined artisans. Democracy did not as yet exist in any practical sense, and there was no right to education, or to equality of opportunity.

Today, by contrast, we have an explosive paradox on our hands: on the one hand, our governments want 80 per cent of young people to leave school with a high standard of leaving qualification; but on the other, in keeping with the ideology of work for work's sake, they want to see an enormous underclass of servants develop to ease the lives and leisure of the better-off classes. What else are those governments doing, in effect, when they reduce taxes on higher incomes on the pretext that alleviating the burden on the rich will create jobs, whilst fiscal transfers in favour of the poorer members of society create hardly any? If, indeed, you increase the resources of the poor, they will merely increase their consumption of current, industrialized products and services, the labour content of which is low. Increasing the disposable income of the rich, by contrast, will increase the consumption of luxury goods and, most importantly, of personal services which have a high labour content, but the economic rationality of which, in overall social terms, is feeble, if not downright non-existent.

In other words, from now on, job creation depends mainly not on *economic* activity, but on *anti-economic* activity; not on the *productive* substitution of waged work for individuals' private production, but on its *counterproductive* substitution. It is no longer the function of job-creation to make savings of working time across society as a whole, but to waste working time for the greater comfort of those who have money to spend. The aim is not to reduce the quantity of work per unit of product or service by maximizing productivity; the aim is now to reduce productivity and maximize the quantity of work by developing a tertiary sector which does not create wealth – what economists delicately describe as "a more employment-rich pattern of growth".

It will perhaps be objected that immense needs remain unmet, and a different distribution of resources would enable us to create millions of public or semi-public jobs which would employ qualified personnel, decently paid, and even offer the less well-off a host of services which they currently lack: assistance to mothers and the aged, home helps, home care, crèches – not to mention organized leisure services, popular or "third age" universities, and so on. All these things can certainly be found in Scandinavia, organized by local authorities, and they provide a great number of jobs, staffed by a workforce that is mainly female. Yet these services, which do not meet needs *for which there is effective economic demand*, obviously cannot be profitable. They do not obey an economic logic. They have to be financed out of taxes – that is, by deductions from the purchasing power of the population. These services are the reason why the rate of taxation in Scandinavia is between 55 and 65 per cent, as opposed to 43 per cent in France.

The Scandinavian model of locally provided household services does, however, raise an even more fundamental question than that of financing: we have to ask to what extent it is right to substitute the services of paid professionals for activities which each of us could just as easily perform ourselves if we had the free time to do so. In other words, to what extent are the needs to which these services are responding themselves the product of a *lack of time*? To what extent would a policy of reducing hours of work – of all work, including household work – reduce not only working time, but also the need to have recourse to professional services, whether provided commercially or otherwise? Would not the thirty-hour, and then the twenty-eight- or twenty-four-hour week, with equitable distribution of domestic tasks between partners, enable service-exchange networks to be organized independently in housing estates, neighbourhoods or local areas, and permit the self-organization of mutual-aid groups based not on money payments but on exchanges of time? By dint of monetizing, professionalizing and transforming into jobs the few remaining production and service activities we still perform for ourselves, might we not reduce our capacity to look after ourselves almost to the point where it disappears, thus undermining the foundations of existential autonomy, not to mention the foundations of lived sociality and the fabric of human relationships?

Lastly, and most importantly, if, as is the tendency today, the governing class defines job-creation as its main aim, where will this transformation of all activities into paid activities (with remuneration as their sole rationale and maximum productivity as their goal) finally end? How long will the extremely fragile barriers which still prevent the professionalization of motherhood or fatherhood be able to hold out? When shall we see the commercial procreation of embryos, the sale of children, or a trade in organs? Are we not already monetizing, professionalizing and selling not only those things and services we *produce*, but also what we *are* and what we cannot produce at will or detach from ourselves? In other words, are we not already transforming ourselves into commodities and treating life as one means among others rather than the supreme end which all means must subserve?

To sum up: the basic problem which confronts us is that of getting beyond the economy and – though this amounts to the same thing – of getting beyond paid work. Economic rationalization frees time, and will continue to do so. Consequently, it is no longer possible to make citizens' income dependent upon the quantity of work the economy requires. It is no longer possible, either, to continue to make paid work the main source of each person's identity, or of their life's meaning.

The casualization of employment and the dualization of society are the perverse forms assumed by the liberation of time which this social system refuses to acknowledge or take into account.

The task of a Left, if there is indeed to be one, consists, then, in transforming this release of time into a new freedom and new rights: the right of everyone, male or female, to earn their living by working, but by working less and less, and better and better, while receiving their full share of the socially produced wealth; and the right to work discontinuously and intermittently, without losing their full income during breaks from work, in such a way as to open up new spaces for activities that have no economic ends and to grant these activities, which are not engaged in for payment, a dignity and a value both for individuals and for society itself.

Notes

1. This paper was delivered to the Cercle Condorcet in Paris in March 1990. An abridged version was published in *Le Monde diplomatique*, June 1990.
2. On this point, see also below, Chapter 9, pp. 102–17.

6

The Crisis of "Work" and

the Post-Industrial Left

The notion of work [*travail*] is an invention of modernity or, more exactly, of industrial capitalism. So long as commodity production remained marginal and the great majority of needs were covered by domestic production and the village economy, the notion of "work" as such (of "*Arbeit schlechthin*", as Marx put it) could not take hold. People "produced", "constructed" and "prepared" things; they "laboured", "toiled", "drudged" and "attended to" a variety of specific "occupations" which had no common measure between them within the framework of the domestic community. And responsibility for the various *activities* was assumed by the husband, the wife, the children or the older members of the family according to an immutable division of labour. These activities were gendered, to borrow Ivan Illich's expression, and there was thus no common denominator between them.[1] They were not interchangeable, and could not be compared and evaluated in terms of a single yardstick. The term "work" referred not to a creative or productive act but to the activity in so far as it entailed pain, annoyance and fatigue.

The notion of work assumed its present meaning only as commodity production and consumption came to gain precedence over production for self. Then "work" became the name of an activity fundamentally different from the activities of subsistence, reproduction, maintenance and care performed within the household. This is not so much because "work" is a paid activity, but because it is done in the public domain and appears there as a *measurable, exchangeable and interchangeable performance*; as a performance which possesses a use-value for others, not simply for the members of the household community carrying it out: *for others in general*, without distinction or restriction, not for a particular, private person.

The modern notion of work thus originally refers to a performance intended for others, possessing utility or use-value for them and hence entitling the person carrying it out to a certain reward or compensation from them. There are two essential characteristics of the notion of work:

1. It must be performed in the public, not the private sphere.
2. It must be intended for others as *social*, not private individuals.

As commodity relations gain ground with industrial capitalism, a third characteristic is added to these two:[2]

3. Work must have a recognized social validity or value, and this will be attested by the possibility of exchanging it for a determinate quantity of *any other kind of work whatever* – or, in other words, by the possibility of selling it, of presenting it as a commodity. It is by its commodity form that it becomes social work "in general", abstract work, participation in the overall social process of production.

It was not until the nineteenth century, when a class of skilled industrial workers appeared, that "work" took on the meaning of creative, "*poietic*" activity which, as the shaping of matter and the mastering of nature, was the source of all wealth.[3] The modern concept of "work", therefore, represents a sociohistorical category, not an anthropological one. "Work" could not function as a concept in any pre-capitalist society. The semantic difficulties one gets into when one seeks to extend the notion of work to all kinds of activities where human relations are to the fore can be appreciated rather clearly from the following passage (with which, in fact, I would entirely concur, were it not for the author's attempt to rescue the socialist ideology of work by a semantic sleight of hand):

> Not liberation *from* work, but the liberation *of* work must be the urgent aim of socialism. And *work* is to be understood here in the sense of *creative activity*, including therefore its non-professional [*nichterwerbsmässig*] forms, such as work-for-oneself, mutual assistance between neighbours, *activity* in self-help groups and charitable projects, etc. By taking advantage of the possibility of meaningful reductions in the hours spent in gainful work [*Erwerbsarbeit*], one can expand the scope for *free activities*; at the same time, the development of *free activities* can make a part of one's professional activities – and hence of one's *gainful* work – superfluous.[4]

Whilst asserting, then, that "work" has to be understood in the sense of "creative activity", the author cannot prevent himself from referring only to professional activities carried out for payment as "work"; non-professional activities and those performed for no economic return are described as "activities", "free activities" or "work-for-oneself" [*Eigenarbeit*]. The point is that if one defines work as "creative activity", then one immediately has the problem of knowing what name to give to work which is not a creative activity, such as the work of supermarket checkout staff, labourers, cleaners, and most of the employees in the service sector, whether public (e.g. postal sorting) or private (waiters or waitresses, data-input personnel). If "liberated work" – "autonomous activity" [*Selbstbetätigung*] in Marx's terminology – is not work in the same sense as the great majority of work carried out on a professional basis for payment, then why apply the term "work" to both? And since, quite clearly, this term is not equally applicable to both, what is the "real", "true" work to which this term applies?

What sense is there, moreover, in speaking of a reduction in working hours if the work whose hours are being reduced is as much a "creative activity" as "free activities", or if, conversely, these latter are work in the same sense as professional occupations? Has the reduction in our working hours no other aim than to allow us to devote to "work" the hours which have been liberated from "work", and thus, in the end, *not to reduce* our working time?

Oskar Negt, one of the writers within the European Left who has devoted the greatest attention to the philosophy of work and time, answers this kind of question by saying that work is "a historical-fundamental category which is tending to become emancipated progressively from the capital relation to become an autonomous activity of transformation of matter".[5] "Work" must therefore be understood, as in Hegel, as the activity by which the human being externalizes his being – that is to say, produces it as a being which exists objectively outside oneself, as "sensuous-practical activity", as "the appropriative shaping of one's own objective world" – hence, in the sense of Greek *poiesis*. For individuals, it is "the means of personal realization", in so far as it "produces non-alienated objects".[6] "Work" thus ostensibly refers here to the non-alienated, autonomously determined activity by which a subject transforms and appropriates the sensible world. To enable that "vital activity" to unfold freely, it is necessary "to expand the space of freedom and reduce the constraints on time".[7]

It is, admittedly, indisputable that "work" in the sense of *poiesis* is a historical–fundamental need: the need the individual feels to appropriate the surrounding world, to impress his or her stamp upon it and, by the objective transformations he or she effects upon it, to acquire a sense of him- or herself as an autonomous subject possessing practical freedom. The question, however, is to what extent this conception of work, handed down to us essentially by the skilled industrial workers of the nineteenth century (workers who were still close to artisan produc-tion, and had a complete grasp of manufacturing *procedures* and the *products* to be made), can apply to the largely de-materialized, pre-determined, specialized work which is the predominant form in today's macro-social space – a form of activity which has no purchase or influence either on the way it is performed or on the final purpose it is to serve, and is commonly referred to simply as "work".

In continuing to apply the idea of work-as-*poiesis* to tasks which in industry, particularly in the service sector, no longer have anything in common with the activities of material transformation and creation carried on by the toolmakers, boilermakers, metal-turners, masons and rolling-mill workers of the nineteenth century, one runs the risk of demanding that today's workers or employees regard as their "means of personal fulfilment" precisely those tasks which prevent such self-fulfilment. The ideology of work, which argues that "work is life" and demands that it be taken seriously and treated as a vocation, and the attendant utopia of a society ruled by the associated producers, play right into the hands of the employers, consolidate capitalist relations of production and domination, and legitimate the privileges of a work elite which, despite the existence of millions of unemployed, views a reduc-tion in working hours which could create extra jobs as incompatible with its professional pride and ethic of productivity.

If one understands the term "work" in the sense of "*poiesis*" or even, as Oskar Negt does at times, in the sense of "*praxis*", the term "work" should not be applied without clearly stated qualification to the immense majority of currently existing jobs and occupations.[8] If work is to be the equivalent of *poiesis*, then real, existing "work" – which, even for highly skilled members of the workforce, is predetermined in its procedures and aims, specialized and de-materialized – is not "true" but "false" work.*

This is not merely a semantic dispute. For as long as a broad stratum of workers could understand their work as the activity by which the human individual realized his being, thanks to the power exerted over matter, it was inherent in the essence of work to seek to emancipate itself from any form of power exerted over the worker. The transformation of work – of *all* work – into an autonomous activity was, according to Marx, the meaning of communism as a lived historical horizon: it was not a distant goal but the lived meaning of the workers' struggles against exploitation, oppression and alienation. Since reification, compulsion

---

* Translator's note: This is a reference to Thomas Schmid's notion of "*falsche Arbeit*". See *Befreiung von falscher Arbeit*, Berlin 1984.

and narrow specialization were negations of the essence of "true" work and the worker as subject, it was impossible for him not to experience his alienation, and not to aspire to free himself from it.

The desire for the liberation of work, for its transformation into autonomous activity, was thus inherent in the essence of true work – and in its alienation. Even when it was alienated, true work rendered the subjects performing it capable of autonomous activity. For them to be able to exercise that *capacity* effectively, only the political conditions which would have allowed them to free themselves from all domination were missing. The *possibility* of transforming work into autonomous activity seemed given; it simply required – and this is a political condition – that the collective appropriation of the means of production be achieved.

In present conditions, by contrast, neither the material possibility nor the subjective capacity for a transformation of work into autonomous activity exists. The labour process and the nature of the tasks performed in work develop the capacity to engage in autonomous activities only in an ever smaller number of employees. That capacity is greater among workers whose origins are in pre-industrial countries (particularly among workers in the building sector and civil engineering) than among modern employees with a technical or multiskilled training. The studies by Horst Kern and Michael Schumann contain illuminating data on this question: technical skills and qualifications do not give rise to a qualified specialist *ability*; workers do not have capacities which they can "objectify in specific performances".[9] This remark applies, *a fortiori*, to intellectual workers, computerized jobs and service personnel. Where individuals are still capable of "sensuous-practical activities impressing their stamp on the material world", they have acquired this capacity, and exercise it, outside their gainful employment. "Work", in the sense of self-realization by the creation of "non-alienated objects", is most often an extra-curricular occupation unrelated to the work at which individuals "earn their living". In short, "true work" is precisely that work we do when we are not "at work". Now, there is no social space in which "true work" – which, depending upon the circumstances, I prefer to call "work-for-oneself" or "autonomous activity" – can deploy itself in such a way as to *produce society* and set its stamp upon it.[10] *It is this space we have to create.* In this regard, a reduction in working hours is a necessary, but not a sufficient, condition.

This brings us to a whole set of politico-strategic questions. If one starts out from a "philosophy of praxis", then there is, at first sight, every reason to hold that the prime goal of a Left trade-union and social politics must be the liberation of work or, in other words, *making possible* the transformation of waged work into autonomous activity. To that end the nature and organization of work, the techniques and procedures, will have to be redefined so as to enable the workers fully to develop, *within* their work, their sensory, bodily and intellectual faculties. Liberation *in* work should therefore precede liberation *from* work – its "reduction to a minimum", as Marx puts it – for only a subject who has already developed his creative capacities will be capable, during his free time, of the autonomous activities on which the "free development of [his] individuality depends" (Marx). This is the argument developed by Oskar Negt, among others:

> If the cultural project is not an integral part of what remains determinant for the unity and meaning of a human life, i.e. material production ..., then society will continue to become culturally impoverished, even if it drastically reduces the hours of compulsory work.[11]

But the question immediately arises: *whose* cultural project is being spoken of here? The position of Oskar Negt, among others, implies that the workers themselves will be able to be the subjects of a cultural redefinition of their work only if that work *already, as of now,* chiefly consists in sensuous-practical activities of productive transformation of matter – in other words, consists in *poiesis*. Now, not only is work in production largely de-materialized and detached from sensory experience, but only a declining minority still work in the sphere of material production. If we accept the principle that "employment and work essentially determine the horizon of my way of seeing the world", *who* is there who can transform work into a fulfilling *poiesis, who* can liberate it in a society where "the way of seeing the world" is "determined" by work that is de-materialized and cut off from sensory experience?[12] Surely not the immense majority of the wage-earning classes. For so long as their work has not been transformed, according to Negt, they will not even have "the capacity for leisure"[13] – that is to say, the "objective and subjective means for occupying the time freed up by autonomous activities".[14]

The problem seems, then, to permit of no solution whatever – so long, at least, as one persists with a strict materialist conception. According to that conception, for the workers to be capable of leisure, their work has first to be transformed; but they will not be able, nor will they desire, to transform their work if they are not already capable of leisure. In other words, the desire for liberation *in* work presupposes a practical experience of autonomy, but the workers are objectively and subjectively denied this by work which deforms and mutilates their sensuous-practical faculties. This was, at one remove, the thesis advanced by Herbert Marcuse when he argued that in the affluent societies, the alienation of individuals is so profound that they are not even able to be conscious of it.

We shall not escape from this vicious circle until we cease to postulate dogmatically that work (real, existing work) is the essential factor of socialization and development of the human faculties – in other words, that individuals are shaped (or determined) by their occupational roles to the point of neither being able, nor desiring, to develop other capacities. Now such is, fortunately, not the case.

Prior to beginning working life, and alongside it, all individuals are exposed to other factors of socialization, other formative experiences and activities. Their faculties, desires and aspirations are not developed *initially* by their professional work. This marks a fundamental difference from the conditions which prevailed in Marx's day. Today, education, training and socialization to a large extent precede the onset of working life, and are not – and do not need to be – linked to carrying on a particular trade or occupation. They also enable a *surplus* of faculties and aspirations to develop which it will not be possible to fulfil in work (as it really exists).

The aspiration to all-round personal development in autonomous activities does not, therefore, *presuppose* a prior transformation of work. The increasingly marked desire, particularly among young people, to be able to find fulfilment in a meaningful and largely self-determined occupation is, above all, the consequence of *the reduction of working time when taken over a lifetime* (working life beginning much later) *and when taken over a year* (more frequent and longer breaks in one's working life), as well as of conditions of employment which less and less often have the stable, regular character of what is still called a "normal job" (i.e. a full-time job for an indefinite number of years, from leaving school to retirement). "A distancing from work, a critical evaluation of whether one's work is really a worthwhile activity, has taken a hold on the consciousness of broad masses of the population," writes Oskar Negt.[15] This sentence says it all: *the old notion of work is no longer valid, the subject assumes a critical distance not only from the product of his work but from that work itself,* regards that work as *something other than his own activity,* other than himself, other than the imprint of his own being on the material on which he works – other than *poiesis.*

It is precisely this type of activity, which is not – or not entirely – my own activity, to which the term "work" refers today. "Work" is distinct from "autonomous activity" and, indeed, from "work-for-oneself". Neither of these latter can any longer be regarded as modes of the former. By "work", we no longer mean all the forms of sensuous-practical activity by which a subject gives objective expression to his or her being, but a particular type of activity which is neither autonomous nor immediately useful to the person performing it. The norm to which everyone now refers in his or her actions is no longer the idea of "work", but that of autonomy and self-fulfilment through a freely chosen activity.[16] It is in the light of this normative idea of personal autonomy and sovereign choice of the way in which one conducts one's life that the reality of work is now evaluated: it is the aspiration to all-round personal development in a non-alienated activity that furnishes the basis of the *critique* of work in the philosophical sense of the term.[17] This is a cultural change – linked, of course, to economic and technical development – which has been a focus for sociological research for some twenty years – at least in the English- and German-speaking countries, and in Scandinavia.

Naturally, I do not mean to suggest by these remarks that we should be indifferent to the nature and forms of work, or leave it to the employers and engineers to determine what they should be. It must be possible for work, its outcomes and aims, working conditions and relations, to be determined and negotiated by the workers themselves. But just as the functioning of complex social systems will never correspond to the intuitive perceptions of lived experience, so the work demanded by complex economic systems can never match up to the lived meaning of autonomous activities carried on for freely determined ends. The division of labour on a macro-social – if not, indeed, a continental or intercontinental – scale always entails a vestige of irreducible alienation and excessively narrow functional specialization. The technical complexity of most end-products, the diversity of technologies combined in them, practically exclude the manufacture from A to Z of complete end-products by self-organized work collectives, freely determining their mode of co-operation, pace and hours of work, production objectives and relations with the end-users. Communities can exert only partial control over processes integrated and co-ordinated at the level of the total social system; they can, at best, expand the space accorded to their influence and initiative; but they cannot eliminate the inertia and rigidities of the system (what Sartre termed the "practico-inert") and its machinery. Negt rightly points out that "self-determination and collective control within the production process" cannot prevent "the ends, namely the production of goods and services, being *pre-given* and thus lying outside the decision-making power of individuals".[18]

Workers' control at the workplace may, to a large extent, "humanize" techniques and tasks, and establish self-managed, *à la carte* working hours, but it cannot effect a return to craft production – that is, to what Negt calls a "world made out of our own objects, objects which we ourselves have produced".

These remarks relating to the material and cultural evolution of work, and of the values which underlie its critical evaluation, explain why I refuse to extend the notion of "work" to autonomous activities and work-for-oneself (i.e. to work which has no use-value except for the person performing it). Reducing working hours will not have a liberating effect, and will not change society, if it merely serves to redistribute work and reduce unemployment. The reduction of working hours is not merely a means of managing the system, it is also an end in itself in so far as it reduces the systemic constraints and alienations which participation in the social process of production imposes on individuals and in so far as, on the other hand, it expands the space for self-determined activities, both individual and collective. This development of free activities which are no longer *work* (in the sense this term has come to assume) obviously cannot be produced simply by reducing working hours. It requires a *politics of time* which embraces the reshaping of the urban and natural environment, cultural politics, education and training, and reshapes the social services and public amenities in such a way as to create more scope for self-managed activities, mutual aid, voluntary co-operation and production for one's own use.

I thus term "work" only such activities as have a place in the *social labour process* and are recognized as forming an integral part of it. These may be socially useful and necessary activities but also forms of unproductive work (for example, servants' work); they may be paid or unpaid (for example, forced labour or prison work). This conception is also shared by Claus Offe and Rolf Heinze:

> Everywhere [an activity] has a use-value for the person who performs it appreciably greater than its utility for other people, the notion of work cannot properly be applied to it, since this latter always presupposes the "social" ... nature of the goals of an activity ... and the *possibility of its critical evaluation* from the point of view of efficiency and productivity.[19]

Work-for-oneself, which we perform in the private sphere (for example, within the household), cannot, therefore, properly be identified as work, since it serves exclusively the maintenance of my own self and those with whom I form a life-community. Such activity retains its proper, intrinsic meaning only if it is not made subject to criteria of social utility; if it is not made to fit into the social labour process, to reproduce or uphold the system of social relations. The lived meaning of the private sphere is to offer a space in which individuals exist for one another as unique persons who do not have to subordinate their lives and their aims to the goals of society, though they may certainly, of their own free will, choose to co-operate on a personal basis in the achievement of social goals.

The conception defended by part of the Left, by some in the women's movement and by Oskar Negt, according to which household activities – particulary maternal activities – are *work* in its supreme form, stands in radical contradiction to the lived sense these activities have in modern societies today. Negt's formulation is particularly illuminating:

> Work in the household . . ., where identity and the capacity to live and love are produced, in order that subjects capable of work may take their place in the system of social labour – i.e. *the true process of the production of life* – is placed at society's disposal *free of charge*, mainly by women.[20]

Autonomous activities and work-for-oneself are thus regarded here as identical with work pure and simple, in the current sense of the term.

In order that women may be presented as the equal of men *within the framework of societies based on work and in terms of the criteria of the ideology of work* (which makes paid work, performed as a part of the social labour process, the essential source of the rights of citizenship and social identity), they are quite simply represented here as *workers in the home.* There they "produce" the capacity to live and the ability to love, they "produce" life, take part in the (social) "process of the production of life" and are thus, as workers, participants in the social labour process, since they do all this "*in order that*" subjects capable of work "may take their place in the system of social labour". In other words, their aim is, and must be, to produce use-values for society in the form of socially useful (capable) labour-powers. It is to this end ("in order that . . .") that women dispense their maternal love. This latter is presented as a service which the mother intentionally offers up to society: it is "placed at society's disposal *free of charge*", which suggests that, in the name of justice and sexual equality, maternal love and the care a mother bestows on her child should be remunerated on the same basis as other examples of socially useful *work*, in conformity with the criteria of social utilitarianism.

In this formulation, the intensely affective and relational bodily activity by which the mother gives a life and cherishes it – a life which takes the incomparably unique form of *her* child – is reduced to women's participation in the social process of production of *life* in general, life as a socially useful product. The relational activity which brings into play the mother's entire sensibility, and all her senses, is bracketed out and reduced to a service rendered to society. This conception, which Oskar Negt (who cannot in any sense be suspected of anti-feminism) takes from certain (Leftist) currents within the women's movement, amounts to *de-feminizing* the biologically, corporeally and affectively specific dimension of motherhood, as though women could gain equality with men only by reducing motherhood to an asexual *job* that has the same nature as male work.[21]

This conception plays right into the hands of the technocratic-authoritarian spirit of domination, since if the production of life and of subjects capable of taking their place in the system of social labour is the truly productive form of *work* from a social point of view, there will be no valid reason not to socialize that work: that is to say, no reason not to remove it from the personal control of each mother and transfer it to socially dependable, functional and efficient apparatuses. This is precisely what is recommended by the advocates of exogenesis (i.e. growing the foetus outside the mother's body right up to total maturation), on the pretext of "releasing women from the servitude of motherhood". Women are to be spared the handicaps pregnancy and childbirth entail for their professional, sporting and social lives so that, in a society where productivity is the supreme value, they may be as "highly efficient" as men. But behind this concern for "competitiveness", there is a hidden agenda: patriarchal society wishes to be rid of each mother's power over *her* child in order not to be dependent on women's decisions, which are always personal ones, as to how many children they wish to bring into the world and the opportune moment at which to have them. This decision has, rather, to be one taken by society, and exogenesis provides the means. This makes it possible to socialize the "maternal function", to rationalize the "process of production of life" in conformity with the needs of the social system. With this measure, de Sade's utopian vision would be fulfilled ("children must belong only to the community"; "it is extremely advantageous to separate them [from their families]").[22]

From a radically eco-feminist and "convivial" point of view, it is admittedly possible, in theory, to defend a conception of work entirely different from the one that is currently accepted. Attempts to do this always present *work* (in the sense of functional insertion in the impersonal process of social labour) as "false" work, and tend to substitute for it personal activities in which individuals have a total grasp of aims and outcomes. On this view, "real" work is auto-production for one's own subsistence, and the "true" economy is that in which individuals control their own means of production, in which the market does not become an alien force independent of individuals – in which, in a word, exchange relations continue to be governed by the traditional, immutable norms of a communitary society. The model implicitly being followed here is that of the old village community, the ashram, the self-sufficient kibbutz: a form of society in which economy and culture, community sphere and private sphere, work and life, are merged, since "work" does not appear as an enforced activity imposed by third parties. What we have here, in fact, are non-capitalist, non-industrial modes of production which are incapable of being industrialized, since primitive accumulation – that is, the production of a surplus required for the expanded reproduction of the means of production (for net productive investment) – is possible only if the producers are *separated* from the means of production. Only such a separation enables workers to be compelled to produce more than *enough*; it alone enables the means of production to function as capital to be increased, and the producers to function as "workers".

The conception of work integrated in community life has served – and continues to serve – as a norm in the definition of the "good life". That norm provides the basis for the radical critiques and condemnations of industrial society. But the reproach Habermas levelled against Hannah Arendt is also valid here: that radical critique remains purely abstract; its only points of reference are medieval or exotic models of society and it cannot draw, within our societies, on any experiences or practical possibilities which would enable it to *be embodied* in acts of social transformation.[23] It is content merely to oppose fundamentally different cultural models to the industrial systems which currently exist. That opposition remains undialectical, ineffective, "utopian" in the bad sense of the word. It simply calls for the whole existing state of things "to be swept away, root and branch". As to *who* might be able to effect such a thing, or when and how, no answer is given; such considerations are disdainfully rejected with a "you just have to ...". It is this practical impotence, this abstract radicalism, which causes the advocates of a return to the agrarian community and subsistence economies ultimately to invoke in support of their case not the normative ethical and political value of their reference model, but the imminence of a catastrophic collapse of industrial civilization: radical de-industrialization is presented as an unavoidable necessity on ecological grounds; only the fraction of humanity converted to it would be able to survive the catastrophe.

To exist politically, an ecological Left has, consequently, an urgent need for *mediations* between the existing industrial system, its wage-workers and its jobs, on the one hand, and, on the other, post-industrial forms of society which comply both with ecological demands and with individuals' aspirations to liberate themselves *from* work as it exists and find *in* work as great a potential for self-determination as possible. We have to start out from what work *is* and what it really means today in order to transform it, reduce it and expand the scope for autonomous activities, production for one's own use, and self-realization for everyone. We shall turn to these questions in the following chapters.

Notes

1. Ivan Illich, *Gender*, London and New York 1983.

2. For more detail, see A. Gorz, *Critique of Economic Reason*, London, 1989, Part II, Chapter 3.

3. Cf. ibid., Part I, Chapters 1 and 2.

4. Johano Strasser, "Sozialismus 2000 oder die Kunst des Möglichen", *Neue Gesellschaft/Frankfurter Hefte* 6, 1990, p. 585 (emphasis added).

5. Oskar Negt, "Aus produktiver Phantasie", in *Wege ins Reich der Freiheit*, Berlin 1989, pp. 69–70.

6. Oskar Negt, *Die Herausforderung der Gewerkschaften*, Frankfurt-am-Main and New York, p. 292.

7. ibid., p. 33.

8. When he writes of "true work" as "living work for common ends", "public work . . . *for* the whole of society", ibid., p. 32.

9. Horst Kern and Michael Schumann, *Das Ende der Arbeitsteilung?*, Munich 1984, p. 277.

10. See Gorz, *Critique of Economic Reason . . .*, pp. 153–71.

11. Negt, *Die Herausforderung der Gewerkschaften*, pp. 180–81.

12. ibid., p. 180.

13. ibid., p. 38.

14. Rainer Land, "Ist wirtschaftliche Entwicklung gestaltbar?", in Michael Brie and Dieter Klein (eds), *Umbruch zur Moderne?*, Hamburg 1991.

15. Negt, *Der Herausforderung der Gerwerkschaften*, p. 266.

16. Of the international research from which this conclusion can be drawn, see particularly Rainer Zoll (ed.), *Nicht so wie unsere Eltern*, Frankfurt-am-Main 1989.

17. On this point, see J. Jessen *et al.*, who describe work-for-oneself as a "niche" in which "aspirations to fully humane work are able to survive", a niche which functions "to lend support to self-awareness and critical capacities", and activates "critical energies in respect of organized waged work within enterprises" (*Arbeit nach der Arbeit. Schattenarbeit. Wertewandel und Industriearbeit*, Opladen 1988, p. 277).

18. The same goes, *a fortiori*, for automated production processes, in which "the behaviour [of the operators] acquires increased importance where the running and outcome of the process are concerned", precisely because "quantity and quality are no longer dependent, in the first instance, on human productive activity, but are the product, first and foremost, of the behaviour of the process and the machinery". In consequence, "the operators' professionalism and their concern for efficiency" must involve "a high degree of identification with the work and the technology, as well as with the predetermined production objectives", write Michael Schumann *et al.* ("Zwischenergebnisse aus dem Trendreport Rationalisierung in der Industrie", *Soziale Welt* 1, 1990). Although they are ostensibly concerned in this article to refute my own arguments on the degree of heteronomy and alienation involved in the largely de-materialized work of process workers, they do therefore recognize in the end that the skills,

initiative and professionalism of the operators of automatic systems are in the *service* of *predetermined* objectives, expressed through the requirements of the machinery and the technical process.

19. Claus Offe and Rolf Heinze, *Organisierte Eigenarbeit*, Frankfurt-am-Main and New York 1990, p. 105. Cf. Gorz, *Critique of Economic Reason* ..., pp. 135ff., 153ff.

20. Negt, *Die Herausforderung der Gerwerkschaften*, p. 32.

21. Cf. Ivan Illich (*Gender*), who demonstrates that the concept of work originally presents this as a "unisex" activity.

22. Cf. Gorz, *Critique of Economic Reason*, pp. 150–52.

23. See Jean-Marc Ferry's remarkable article, "Habermas, critique de Hannah Arendt", *Esprit*, 6, June 1980, pp. 109–24.

7

Old and New Actors in the

Central Conflict

In the developed late-capitalist societies the reality of class as organized power is destroyed on the terrain of class society.

DETLEV CLAUSSEN[1]

Everyday solidarity is based on the search for open communication free of domination. It is, therefore, from the first, more comprehensive than workers' solidarity; it does not have the latter's constantly re-emerging limitations, indeed it even has universalist tendencies.

RAINER ZOLL[2]

1. The socialist movements, and later the socialist parties, developed out of the struggle against the exploitation and oppression of the wage-earning masses and the battle against the social goals and conceptions of the bourgeois ruling strata. The socialist project of a new society at first contained two elements.

- On the one hand, there was the claim to leadership by a class of skilled workers, which experienced its ability to control the production process itself in its daily practice. It was determined to seize power from the class of owners, whom it regarded as parasites and exploiters, in order to place the development of the productive forces at the service of emancipation and human needs.

- On the other hand, there was the resistance of a disenfranchised and oppressed proletariat of women, children and men who toiled in workshops and factories at starvation wages, and had to fight for their political and economic rights. These unskilled labouring masses could achieve the cultural and social perspectives with which to overcome oppression only through an alliance with the skilled workers. Conversely, the potential leading class of skilled workers in part drew legitimation for its claim to leadership from the unbearable immiseration of the proletarian masses, for whom the elimination of capitalist domination was a question of life and death; however, legitimation was also provided by man's domination of the forces of nature, embodied in the worker – above all in the versatile craft worker. The real subject of this domination was the worker himself, not only as "collective worker", but also as individualized bearer of irreplaceable human capacities and human skills.

2. Beyond the historicity of the central conflict between labour and capital, however, socialism signified more than its manifest political and social contents: more than emancipation of the disenfranchised, oppressed and exploited; more than just the claim to power of the immediate masters of nature. Resistance and the claim to power of the working class contained a fundamental critique, not only of the capitalist relations of production, but also of capitalist rationality itself, as expressed in commodity, market and competitive relationships.

Actions are economically rational in so far as they aim at the maximization of productivity. But this becomes possible only on two conditions: (1) Labour has to be separated from the personal singularity of the labourer and must be expressed as a calculable and measurable quantity; and (2) The economic goal of the maximization of productivity cannot be subordinated to any non-economic social, cultural or religious goals; it must be pursued ruthlessly. Only unlimited competition in a free market makes such ruthlessness possible – indeed, enforces it. Only the "free market economy" permits economic rationality to make itself independent of the demands of sociality, in which it is embedded in all non-capitalist societies, and to withdraw from society's control – in fact, even to enrol society in its service.

The socialist workers' movement came into being as the positive negation of capitalist development. To the principle of the maximization of productivity, it counterposed the necessary self-limitation of the amount of labour performed by the workers; to the principle of competitive struggle between isolated individuals, it counterposed the principle of solidarity and mutual support, without which self-limitation would be practically impossible. The socialist workers' movement aimed, therefore, to set limits to economic rationality, and ultimately to make that rationality serve the needs of a humane society.

The Central Conflict

The central conflict out of which the socialist movement has developed revolves, then, around the expansion or limitation of the areas in which economic rationality is allowed to evolve unhindered in market and commodity relations. It is characteristic of capitalist society that relations conducive to the valorization of capital predominate in the hierarchy of values, in everyday life and in politics. The socialist movement opposes this with the striving after a society in which the maximization of productivity and profit is locked into a total social framework in such a way that it is subordinated to non-quantifiable values and goals, and that economically rational labour no longer plays the principal role in the life of society or of the individual. Socialism, understood as the transcendence of economic rationality, assumes, consequently, that this rationality has already fully evolved. Where, in the absence of market and commodity relations, it has not yet established itself, "socialism" cannot set economic rationality in the service of a social project intended to transcend it. Where "socialism" is conceived as the planned development of as yet non-existent economic structures, it inevitably turns into its opposite: it subordinates society to the accumulation of capital, and posits economic rationality as the objective around which social life is to be reorganized. Such a society cannot assert its independence of economic rationality. It is "economicized" through and through.

3. The central conflict over the extent and limits of economic rationality has lost nothing of its sharpness and historical significance. If one understands socialism as a form of society in which the demands deriving from this rationality are subordinated to social and cultural goals, then socialism remains more relevant than ever. Nevertheless, the concrete historical contents, as well as the actors in the central conflict, have changed. That conflict used to be conducted, culturally and politically, at the level of workplace struggles; it has gradually spread to other areas of social life. Other kinds of antagonism have been superimposed on the contradiction between living labour and capital, and have relativized it. The striving after emancipation, after fulfilment in activities freely chosen, and to shape one's own life cannot assert itself without trade-union struggles for a reshaping of work and conditions of work, but it also demands actions on other levels and on other fronts, which may be equally – and at times even more – important. The question as to the "subject" that will decide the central conflict, and in practice carry out the socialist transformation, cannot, consequently, be answered by means of traditional class analysis.

4. In Marxian analysis, the class of skilled workers was destined to rule over a totality of productive forces, so that a totality of human capacities would develop in each worker. The fully developed individual would consequently resist every external determination, take command of the production process, and set himself the goal of the "free development of individuality" within and outside productive co-operation.

Now, unfortunately, actual developments have not confirmed these predictions. Although in parts of industry a "recomposition of complex tasks" (Kern and Schumann) is becoming possible or even necessary, there can be no question – even in the case of the new, versatile, skilled production workers – of a totality of skills being developed to command a totality of productive forces. The recomposed task always affects only the manufacture of parts of an end-product (for example, of crankshafts, cylinder heads, gearboxes) or of their assembly and control. As a consequence of its ever greater complexity, the total social production process demands a functional specialization of tasks in all areas. Max Weber spoke in this context of *Fachmenschentum* (specialized mankind). But specialization always stands in contradiction to the free all-round development of individual capacities, even if it demands initiative, responsibility and personal commitment to the job. A computer specialist, a maintenance worker, a chemicals worker or a postman cannot feel themselves to be – and develop themselves in their work as – creative human beings, materially shaping with hand and mind the world experienced through their senses. They can succeed in doing so only outside their professional employment. Specialization – that is, the social division of labour beyond the level of the individual plant – renders the production process opaque. In the course of their work the operatives can hardly have any influence on the decisions which relate to the character, determination, use-value and social utility of the end-products. A process worker is in no way different, according to Oskar Negt, from the civil servant in a public body, who is also responsible only for sections of work cycles and for the precise execution of tasks that are placed before him. He makes a contribution to the functioning of areas about which, as a rule, he knows nothing.[3]

The concept – which first appears in Hegel and is subsequently taken over by Marx – according to which labour is the material shaping of the world experienced by the senses, through which man becomes the producer of himself, was still valid seventy years ago for the overwhelming majority of the working class: they were employed in non-formalized activities in which individual know-how, physical strength, planning and self-organization of the sequence of tasks played a decisive role. Today the majority of wage-earners work in administration, banks, shops or transport, in postal, caring and education services, where individual performance is usually not measurable, and labour has lost its materiality.

There is no way that the "modern workers" who have now supplanted the old versatile skilled workers can question the meaning and social purpose of production on the basis of their intuitive understanding of their work or the power it confers on them. The transformation of the technical power exerted within the production process into political power within society can no longer be effected through the workers' identification with their function. It requires, rather, that they distance themselves from the work role allotted to them, that they see that role within the context of the social system. A capacity to achieve such a perspective is at least potentially inherent in the socialization of these modern workers, since this does not primarily take the form of learning an occupational role. Indeed, professional training develops capacities which are never utilized to the full within labour. This may require a sense of responsibility and independence, but always only to fulfil predetermined functions: it demands "autonomy within heteronomy".

However, to have the *capacity* fundamentally to question capitalist relations of production is not the same as having the *possibility* of doing so. That possibility cannot be realized by the worker as such at the workplace (one thinks of maintenance specialists in automated plants, of employees in nuclear power stations or in the chemical industry), but only in their capacity as citizens, as consumers, as tenants, or as the users of private and public facilities – that is, as participants in social relations beyond the workplace and members of a much larger community.

New Cultures of Resistance

It can or should be the task of trade-union work to encourage this sense of a wider belonging, responsibility and solidarity, and the related distancing from a predetermined occupational role. However, this clearly implies a changed conception of trade unionism. Its role would then no longer consist *solely* in representing and defending the interests of modern workers *as such*, but *also* in providing them with the possibility of seeing their occupational activity in relation to an economic and political development shaped by the valorization of capital. This can take many forms, such as working groups; public discussions and critical investigations regarding the social and political implications of techno-logical innovations and their effect on the environment. "What may be advantageous to the employees of one company," writes Hinrich Ötjen, "may under certain circumstances involve disadvantages or reduced future opportunities for others", and he continues:

If the trade unions want to remain relevant, then at the very least a public debate on such conflicts of interest should be organized at a local level; otherwise new movements, which offer the workers the possibility of voicing their various interests, will be more relevant to them than the trade unions. Up to now, trade-union immobility has frequently given workers cause to set up citizens' initiatives; they are discouraged by the difficulties they encounter when they try to organize such a debate within the trade union.[4]

The important point, then, is that for workers in the modern sectors, criticism of capitalism and a socialist sensibility are not to be derived from their working lives or their class consciousness but, rather, from the discovery they make as citizens, parents, consumers, residents of a neighbourhood or town, of capitalist development dispossessing them of their – social and natural – lifeworld. Thus it is neither their occupational capacities nor their identification with their jobs which will shape their resistance to that dispossession, but their lives and experience outside work.

This is very much the argument advanced by Alain Touraine.[5] According to him, the central conflict is no longer the antagonism between living labour and capital, but that between the large scientific-technical-bureaucratic apparatuses, which I – following Max Weber and Lewis Mumford – have called the "bureaucratic–industrial mega-machine", and a population which feels itself robbed of the possibility of shaping its own life by external determination of its interests, by professional know-alls, and by technological appropriation of the environment. However, nothing should prevent one recognizing the bureaucratic–industrial megamachine and its leading stratum as also the expression of an economic rationality characteristic of capitalism, which takes the shape of industrial growth, the valorization of ever larger quantities of capital, the monetization and professionalization of social and interpersonal relations.

5. The inadequacy of an analysis that relies principally on the cultural resistance to the "colonization of the lifeworld" contained in the "new social movements" is, in my view, that these movements do not consciously and concretely attack the domination of the economic rationality embodied in capitalism. These movements are certainly anti-technocratic – that is, directed against the cultural hegemony of the leading stratum of the ruling class – but they strike only at the cultural assumptions and social consequences of the relations of domination, not at their economic-material core. The new social movements will become the bearers of socialist transformation when they ally themselves not only

with the "modern worker" but also with the contemporary equivalent of the disenfranchised, oppressed and immiserated proletariat – that is, with the post-industrial proletariat of the unemployed, occasionally employed, short-term or part-time workers, who neither can nor want to identify themselves with their job or their place in the production process. Estimates that this group is likely to make up 50 per cent of the active population in the 1990s are beginning to seem realistic: in West Germany, as in France, more than half the workers newly started in recent years are employed in precarious or part-time jobs. Workers who are employed in this way already constitute in total more than a third of the wage-earning population. Together with the unemployed, that makes a "post-industrial proletariat" of 40 to 45 per cent in Great Britain, and in the United States as much as 45 to 50 per cent. The two-thirds society has already been left behind.[6]

Now it would be a mistake to see in the 40 per cent excluded from normal full-time employment only people who hanker after a full-time job. In its most recent research related to the demand for a thirty-five-hour week, the Italian metal workers' union, Fiom-CGIL, reaches the same conclusion as similar studies in France and West Germany. According to this:

> we are engaged in a process of social change as a result of which work now occupies only a minor place in people's lives. More precisely, work – paid work – is losing its central position, though it is more a question of a decline of the socialization function of work than of a refusal to work. Work is valued only when it has the quality of autonomous creative activity. Otherwise it is regarded merely as a way of earning a living, and for women also as a way of achieving independence from the family.[7]

Rainer Zoll also came to similar conclusions as a result of exhaustive research, with reference above all to young people. He concludes that "the break-up of the old identity structures" throws young people back on themselves "in their search for an identity of their own". They could never achieve the permanent, stable identity that is produced by traditional craft skills being handed down from father to son and mother to daughter; they have to build up an identity through "communicational" relations, and that identity, based on "self-realization", will always be an open one, and subject to modification. The choice of professions potentially available to a young person is greater than ever, but the chances of actually finding what she or he was looking for – namely a job with creative and socially useful aspects in which she or he could realize him- or herself – is extremely limited. The number of such jobs is estimated at 5 per cent. It is therefore understandable that many have already given up the race before it has even begun. The obvious consequence of this situation is that individuals transferred the search for self-realization to other terrains.[8] It should therefore be no surprise that, according to an Italian survey which now dates back quite a few years, young people frequently prefer to take part-time work, to enter precarious or short-term work situations, and to pursue if possible, by turns, a variety of activities; even among university students with limited means, the professional activity most frequently preferred was that which left most time for one's own cultural activities.[9] The impossibility of creating stable, socially useful, and economically rational full-time jobs for almost half the wage-earning population is matched, therefore, by the desire among a significant proportion of younger wage-earners not to be tied, either full-time or for life, to a career or job which only very rarely makes use of all their personal capacities in a fulfilling way.

Limiting the Sphere of Economic Rationality

Now what connects this post-industrial proletariat of wage-earners who cannot identify themselves with their position in the productive process with the "modern worker"? Both strata experience the fragility of a wage relation based on measurable work performance. It is the case, both for those not working full-time or all the year round, or those who are precariously employed, and for the core workforces of "modern workers", that their effective labour is not constantly required. The first group is needed for limited, usually short-term, foreseeable units of time; the second is needed for situations that are frequently quite unpredictable, which can occur several times a day or only relatively seldom. "Process workers", maintenance specialists, and also firemen or caring professionals must be constantly available, and in an emergency also work twenty hours without a break. They are paid for their availability, not only for their performance. They are on duty even when they are not active. In the case of the precariously employed, by contrast, only that time is paid during which they are performing effective work, even though it is of the utmost importance to industry and services that flexible, willing and capable labour should be available at short notice. It is for exactly this reason that the demand of the precariously employed – usually working less than six months a year – that they also be paid for their availability during interruptions of the wage relation, which are no fault of theirs but advantageous to business, is quite legitimate.

It is therefore a question of uncoupling income from work *time*, not income from work itself. This demand is altogether rational since, as a consequence of increases in productivity through technical innovation, the total economic production process requires less and less labour. Under these circumstances it is absurd to continue to make the wages paid out by the economy as a whole dependent on the volume of labour performed, and the individual income dependent on individually performed work time. Work time as the basis for the distribution of socially produced wealth is clung to solely for reasons of ideology and political domination. For the post-industrial proletariat that is not employed full-time or all the year round, the wage relation becomes the manifest expression of a relation of domination whose previous legitimacy derived from the now untenable rationality of the work ethic. The common goal of the "modern workers" and the post-industrial proletariat is to free themselves from this domination. However, this goal is pursued by them in very different ways. For the post-industrial proletariat of marginal workers, it is principally a matter of being able *to transform the frequent interruptions to their wage–labour relationship into a new freedom*; that is, to be entitled to periodic unemployment instead of being condemned to it. For this purpose they need the right to a sufficient basic income which permits new lifestyles and forms of self-activity. For the core workforces of "modern workers", as for others with full-time jobs, forms of control over working time, such as self-determined flexibility of working hours or even linear reductions in the length of the working week, may seem more attractive.

This may appear to be a new form of the earlier social stratification, with its distinction between skilled workers on the one side and proletariat on the other. As in earlier times, the contemporary proletariat is rebelling principally against the arbitrariness of relations of domination that express themselves in the absurd compulsion to live from wage-labour of which not enough is available; while autonomy within and outside professional life becomes the main desire of "modern workers". The divisions between the two strata are consequently much more fluid than they may first appear to be, and could to a great extent be removed. Progressive general reductions in working hours must logically lead to a redistribution of work, whereby *the skilled jobs would be made available to a much larger number of wage-earners*; and at the same time *the right to – and possibility of – interruptions of the wage–labour relation could be made available to everyone*. An alliance of both strata does indeed seem feasible, especially on the demand for reduced working hours, provided that such a demand does not become a straitjacket but enhances autonomy within and outside labour.

Reduction in the average annual working time, or even in the quantity of labour performed in the course of four or six years, entitling the wage-earner to an undiminished income, offers in this respect the greatest scope and possibilities of choice. The thirty-hour week, for example, whose achievement the trade unions and left-wing parties of most European countries have set themselves as a goal, corresponds to an annual working time of approximately 1,380 hours and, combined with the right to a sabbatical year, an average of approximately 1,150 hours annually. A society that no longer needs all its labour-power full-time and all the year round can also easily provide for reductions in working hours, without loss of income, in the form of the right to longer breaks from work. Until the beginning of the twentieth century, journeymen and skilled workers always took this right. Variety, tramping, collecting experiences, were for them part of human dignity. Consequently, a reduction in working time must be regarded "not only as a technocratic means to a more just distribution of work" which allows everyone to acquire an indisputable right to their share of social wealth, "but as the society-transforming goal of procuring more 'disposable time' for human beings".[10] This time may be used however one likes, depending on one's situation in life, to experiment with other lifestyles or a second life outside work. In any case, it limits the sphere of economic rationality. It has a socialist significance in so far as it is combined with a social project that puts economic goals in the service of individual and social autonomy.

Jacques Delors has pointed out that forty years ago a twenty-year-old worker had to be prepared to spend a third of his or her waking life at work. Today his or her working hours amount only to a fifth of his or her waking time, and they are set to shrink further. From the age of fifteen, one spends more time in front of the television today than at work.[11] If a socialist movement does not focus on cultural, interpersonal, community life as intensively as it does on working life, it will not be able to succeed against the capitalist leisure and culture industry. It has a chance only if it consciously insists on the creation of expanding free spaces for the development of a many-sided, communicative, everyday culture and everyday solidarity liberated from commodified relations of buying and selling.

6. The expansion of areas freed from economic calculation and imma-nent economic necessities cannot mean that a socialist *economy* or alternative *economy* is taking the place of the capitalist one. There is no other science of management – no other micro-economic rationality – than the capitalist one. The question is solely to what extent the criteria of economic rationality should be subordinated to other types of rationality both within and beyond companies. Capitalist economic rationality aims at the greatest possible efficiency, which is measured by the "surplus" obtained per unit of circulating and fixed capital. Socialism

must be conceived as the binding of capitalist rationality within a democratically defined framework, which should serve the achievement of democratically determined goals, and also, of course, be reflected in the limitation of economic rationality within companies.

Consequently, there can be no question of dictating to public or private companies conditions which make the calculation of real costs and performance impossible, or which are incompatible with initiatives aiming at economic efficiency, and consequently prevent economically rational company management. If it is to have general validity – which on the grounds of justice it must have – reduction in working time cannot take place purely at the individual company level and be dependent on a particular company's increases in productivity. The compensation for wage reductions as a result of a general reduction in working hours, guaranteed to all, can also not be financed by a general taxation on increases in company productivity (machine tax), but must be guaranteed by indirect taxes, applicable to every European Community country, which are cost-neutral for the businesses and do not affect competitiveness. But that is already another chapter.

Translated by Martin Chalmers and Chris Turner

Notes

1. Detlev Claussen, "Postmoderne Zeiten", in H.L. Krämer and C. Leggewie (eds), *Wege ins Reich der Freiheit*, Berlin 1989, p. 51.

2. Rainer Zoll, "Neuer Individualismus und Alltagssolidarität", in ibid., p. 185.

3. Oskar Negt, *Lebendige Arbeit, enteigneite Zeit*, Frankfurt 1984, p. 188.

4. Hinrich Ötjen, *Krise der Gewerkschaften*, MS, Hattingen 1989.

5. Alain Touraine, *Return of the Actor*, trans. J. Myrna Godzich, Minneapolis 1988.

6. W. Lecher, "Zum zukünftigen Verhältnis von Erwerbsarbeit und Eigenarbeit aus gewerkschaftlicher Sicht", *wsi Mitteilungen* 3, 1986, p. 256.

7. According to the report by Bruno Vecchi in *Il Manifesto*, 1 July 1989.

8. Rainer Zoll, *Nicht so wie unsere Eltern? – Ein neues kulturelles Modell?*, Opladen and Wiesbaden, 1988.

9. S. Benvenuto and R. Scartenazzi, "Verso la fine del giovanilismo", *Inchiesta*, November–December 1981, p. 72.

10. Peter Glotz, "Die Malaise der Linken", *Der Spiegel* 51, 1987.

11. Jacques Delors, *Our Europe*, London 1992, p. 107.

8

Which Way is Left?

Social Change in the

Post-Industrial Age

*Interview with John Keane**

Keane: You've been arguing for ten years or more that full employment is a thing of the past, that it has become economically impossible as a result of a set of technical transformations that are also known as the "micro-electronics revolution". In your view, Keynes is dead: full employment will not be re-established by stimulating economic growth. Don't recent developments in both the United States and Europe show this argument to be ill-founded?

Gorz: It all depends on what you mean by "full employment". In the past, the term referred to a situation in which everyone could find a full-time job, lasting all year, from the time they left school until they retired. We shall never see that again. In all the industrially developed countries, between 40 and 50 per cent of the active population are in what is called "atypical" employment – precarious, part-time, temporary, or short-term jobs with periods of unemployment in between. This is as true in Western Europe as in the United States.

The "death of Keynes" was announced as long ago as the early 1970s in a study by the German metalworkers' union in Frankfurt, which showed that robotization not only reduces the amount of labour required but also saves capital. In other words, the more you invest in industry, the more jobs you eliminate, and that includes jobs in the engineering industries. The "productivity of capital" increases alongside the productivity of labour. *Fortune* magazine has published several studies of individual enterprises illustrating this fact, most notably one dated 25

Translator's note: This interview, which was carried out in 1990, was first published in *Grand Street* 38, New York 1991.

May 1987, on the Japanese firm Fanuc, where the manufacture of robots has itself been robotized. In one of its entirely automated plants, "70 workers and 130 robots produce 18,000 motors a month. The plant cost $32 million, which is around a tenth of what a conventional factory would have cost, and it requires only one-tenth as many workers."

Keane: Many economists would argue that you exaggerate the importance of productivity gains. They say these are happening much more slowly overall than in the 1960s, and the problem is not that they are too rapid but that they are insufficient.

Gorz: Statistically, that's right. But you have to see why. You have, roughly speaking, two sectors in modern economies. In the first of these, the microelectronics revolution is bringing very rapid productivity gains. These are distinctly more rapid than in the past, in the order of 10 to 12 per cent per year in the automotive industry, for example. In the second sector, which covers services that cannot be industrialized (personal services, teaching, advertising, decorating, etc.), productivity is progressing slowly or not at all. Now, as a direct result of increasing productivity, the number of workers in the first sector is constantly falling, whereas the number in the second sector is rising, because that is the only place where extra jobs can be created, one way or another.

Twenty years ago, workers in industry represented something like 40 per cent of the workforce in West Germany, Italy, and Great Britain. When the productivity of labour increased by 7 per cent in industry and by 2 per cent in other activities, it grew by 4 per cent within the economy as a whole. Currently, workers in industry represent barely 30 per cent of the working population. Now, even if their productivity increased by nearly 10 per cent, the 4 per cent rise in overall annual productivity would be reached only if the productivity of services also rose, for its part, by 1.5 to 2 per cent. But such a rise is quite out of the question, because the main function of the very high – and constantly growing – proportion of services is to create jobs for people who would otherwise be unemployed, even if the jobs created are totally irrational from the economic point of view. That is what I have called the "tertiary anti-economy", since its objective is to ensure that a maximum amount of paid labour is consumed, while the modern economy has the opposite goal, seeking to reduce the quantity of labour required per unit of production.

If, for example, you take the jobs created in the last ten years or so in the United States, you will find that most of these jobs have the following function: the two hours you used to spend mowing your lawn, walking your dog, going to fetch your paper, doing your housework, or looking after your children are transferred to a service-provider who does those tasks in your stead, for payment. That person does nothing that you couldn't do yourself. He or she merely frees up two hours of your time by enabling you to buy two hours of his or her time. This type of transfer is the essential characteristic of servants' work, and even the founding fathers of political economy insisted that work done by servants is economically unproductive. Moreover, this type of employment develops only in conditions of extreme inequality. The new servants offer their services to private individuals because they can't find jobs within the social process of production, and it's in the interest of private individuals to buy other people's time only if two hours of their own working time bring in distinctly more than they pay for two hours of the servants' time. The "service society", based on the development of personal services, is necessarily a "dual society".

Keane: Yet neo-liberals suggest that the technological revolution will have universally beneficial effects if only it is allowed to proceed unhindered. They defend policies designed to loosen market rigidities and abolish state regulations on employees and investors. "Be flexible or perish" is the new motto, and we're now seeing an unprecedented cult of private enterprise bravely battling for its full market share.

Gorz: But the microelectronics revolution wasn't launched by private enterprise. Its origins lie in the billions of dollars of public money invested by the American government in its military and space programme. In Japan, where it developed most quickly, that technological revolution was promoted voluntarily by the Ministry of International Trade and Industry, working together with industry and the big banks. Microprocessors, biotechnologies, and nuclear and photovoltaic energy were all based initially on research and development financed by the state. In Europe, even industrial giants like Philips and Siemens agreed to take on the joint development of a 4-megabyte "chip" only on condition that they receive public funding for it.

Neo-liberals always argue as if capital were invested spontaneously where unsatisfied needs are at their greatest. This has never been the case. Capital is invested where it can be sure of the highest returns. Producing to meet the most pressing needs of the needier sections of the population is never the best way to make the most money. The way to do that is to produce goods or services likely to appeal to the most prosperous strata. That is why the liberalization of the economy always begins by impoverishing the poor and enriching the rich. This was obvious in the last century and it is again today, not only in Bush's America or Thatcher's Britain, but also throughout the rest of Europe. If you examine the sectors in which exacerbated competition between enterprises is speeding up technical innovation, improving product quality, and increasing productivity, you mainly find products aimed at the most prosperous segment of the population, while the standard of living of the people at the bottom of the wage ladder is continually deteriorating, as are their living conditions.

The free play of market mechanisms leads, then, to social decline, and contrary to what many neo-liberals argue, that social decline is not accompanied by economic boom. In fact, the opposite is true. The three European countries that have the most efficient economies and the highest technical standards – Sweden, Switzerland, and West Germany – are precisely the ones where strong trade-union power makes the labour market more rigid, hinders price competition, and maintains higher wages and better working conditions than elsewhere. Taking everything into account, wage costs are 30 per cent higher there than in France and 50 per cent higher than in Britain. And that is why the productivity of labour and the rate of innovation are highest there. It is much more difficult in these countries – particularly in Sweden – to hire and fire temporary workers, so Swedish companies are forced to make unparalleled efforts to train their workforces and reorientate their production. The result is that the Swedish economy is probably the most flexible and efficient in the world. Where it is relatively easy to take on and lay off temporary workers and to employ a very low-cost workforce, as in Britain or France, technical innovation is less rapid and product quality lower.

Keane: In all the countries of Europe, from the Atlantic to the Urals, virtually everyone today is in favour of the unhindered play of market mechanisms. Yet in your writings you argue for an increasing restriction of the sphere of commodity exchange. You are one of the few still to claim a central role for planning and for public control of macro-economic decisions. But aren't market mechanisms, contrary to what Marx thought, something more than – and other than – characteristics of "bourgeois" society? Aren't they necessary to some extent, if only to prevent shortages and bottlenecks? And doesn't the idea of abolishing commodity relations to make room for the self-management of production and exchange bear the imprint of last century's egalitarian utopias, which simply cannot be translated into reality?

Gorz: You are quite right that there can be no complex society without commodity relations or markets. The total abolition of market relations would presuppose the abolition of the social division and specialization of labour, and thus the return to autarkic communities or a society of kibbutzim. Ursula Le Guin conjured up a planetary kibbutz of this kind in her novel *The Dispossessed*, which is the most striking description I know of the seductions – and snares – of self-managed communist or, in other words, anarchist society.

But we have to be clear first of all about what the terms "commodity relations", "free competition", and "market economy" mean. "Commodity relations" means exchanges based on buying and selling in which what is being bought or sold takes the commodity form. You sell to me, I pay you, we are quits, and our relationship can end there. I have shown elsewhere that this buying and selling relationship is rational and functional only when the output of the object or service being sold is measurable, and where it therefore lends itself to quantitative evaluation. If it includes personal involvement, a "gift of oneself", it is no longer possible to be quits by paying for it, whatever the price paid. It impoverishes and depersonalizes the fabric of emotional life and human relationships if commodity relations and monetarization are extended to the furnishing of non-quantifiable goods and services, which achieve their purpose only if money is not their goal. The more we extend the sphere of activities about which we can say "This is not for sale" or "I can't put a price on this", the richer are our individual and social lives.

Yet the existence of commodity relations does not necessarily imply the existence of a real market. Goods can be bought and sold at prices set by convention, in conformity with centuries-old tradition, or at prices fixed by the state. In this latter case, competing sellers do not directly confront buyers seeking to buy at the best price. The sellers are not, therefore, forced by competition to seek maximum productivity of the factors of production. This has advantages as well as disadvantages, as Max Weber and Karl Polanyi – not to mention Plato and the Christian theologians – have shown.

Lastly, there may be commodity relations and competition on markets without there being a true market economy. And indeed, you made the distinction yourself in speaking of "market mechanisms" without using the term "market economy". The fact is that the market economy is an economy in which prices are established freely, in every sector, at a level where supply and demand reach equilibrium, without intervention or manipulation or hindrance of any kind. Do you know a single country whose economy is regulated in that way?

Keane: The answer is certainly no, except for the land of pure capitalism that exists in the heads of certain neo-liberals.

Gorz: If the price of agricultural produce or the level of wages were determined by the laws of supply and demand, most of us would long ago have died of starvation. In all the industrial nations, the relative prices of goods and services are regulated by the state; if they weren't, society wouldn't be viable. Everything that's vital is subsidized: agricultural production, housing, health, transport, education, libraries, research, museums, theatres, and so on. And the rest is taxed to varying degrees by a system of VAT or specific taxes – on petroleum products, alcohol, tobacco and matches, and so on. The more extensive the sphere of commodity relations, the more the state has to intervene in the market mechanisms to correct and regulate their functioning. The fact is that the market is, by definition, the outcome of the activities of individuals each pursuing his or her own immediate interests. Thus a higher authority, the state, is required to take responsibility for defending the general interest, including the existence of a market system.

Keane: This brings us to the fundamental question: To what extent must market mechanisms be allowed free play?

Gorz: This is the question that has been at the heart of political conflict for two hundred years. Commodity relations, by which I mean the freedom of each individual to pursue his or her own immediate interests, tend to destroy both civil society and the general conditions that make them possible. The nature and extent of the advantages that an individual has the right to procure for him- or herself must therefore be restricted by law. The history of capitalism is the history of a continual extension of these legal restrictions: the abolition of slavery; anti-monopoly and anti-trust legislation; the prohibition of the sale of children and women; the prohibition of child labour; Sunday as a rest day; the ten-hour and then the eight-hour working day; the legal minimum wage; legal standards for quality, safety, hygiene and pollution; universal health insurance; old age pensions; and so on.

The basic problem is that this way of limiting and correcting market mechanisms does not prevent the destruction of civil society. The welfare state can, to a certain extent, limit the scope of that destruction, but overall it functions as a substitute for a civil society that is in the process of withering away. In some respects, it even hastens the process of decay. I'm entirely in agreement with the way you treat this question in *Democracy and Civil Society*: there can't be socialism without democracy, and there can't be democracy without a much more substantial civil society comprising a set of self-organized public activities recognized and protected by the state. Socialism was born out of a conflict between civil society and the market. It took off as a movement by demanding that market forces be contained, subdued and controlled by society, whereas capitalism presented the opposite demand. However, for society to control market forces and place economic rationality in the service of societal and cultural ends, it is necessary, first, that society have an autonomous existence; and second, that the market exist or has existed, and that economic agents have been coerced by it into economically rational behaviour – that is, the pursuit of maximum efficiency in putting the factors of production to work.

For us, in the capitalist countries, the first point is the most important. It implies that a socialist politics cannot be content merely to correct and regulate the operation of the market through state controls and services financed by the state. It must promote the development of a sphere of lived sociality (what the Germans call *soziale Lebenswelt*) made up of forms of self-organized, voluntary co-operation and of non-commodity, non-monetary exchange. It must promote the social control of markets by citizens working together, and not merely by the public authorities. The question of what must be produced and how, the question of social priorities, of models of consumption, of styles of life – all this is currently decided by technocrats, businessmen and bankers. Socialism would have to mean the democratization of these decisions, their public discussion at the level of associations, trade unions, movements, public hearings, and elected assemblies; and it would also have to mean taking into account criteria with which technocrats and company directors do not normally concern themselves.

Keane: When you call for social forms of control of markets, that implies you've given up the idea of a planned public sector, which you advocated in the past, at least for the production of necessities.

Gorz: In the 1960s, planning was all the fashion. Today all forms of planning and public ownership are condemned, both in the East and in the West. Currently the "market" is in vogue, and is supposed to provide the necessary regulation and adjustments in an ideal way. This doesn't hold water. A complex economy cannot do without certain forms of planning. And planning is not incompatible either with the existence of markets or with the most varied forms of ownership, whether these be public, private, co-operative or municipal.

If you rely solely on private initiative, on the market, you get into blind alleys. In China, for example, thousands of entrepreneurs all over the place set about manufacturing refrigerators, which is relatively easy and very profitable in the short run, only to find that the steel industry didn't produce enough sheet metal, since you can't set up the plants for producing that overnight; it requires long-term investment and infra-structures that depend on public funding. No industry, no large- or medium-scale enterprise, can dispense with planning its amortization, its investments, its labour needs, its purchases of raw materials and components several years ahead, and co-ordinating its plans with industries further up the line, and with the public authorities. And the same obviously goes for public services such as education, transport, insurance, roads, and water distribution. Or for agricultural production, in which the free operation of the market and individual initiative lead, as in the four-year pig cycle, to overproduction with a collapse of prices, followed by shortages and skyrocketing prices, and so on. These cyclical fluctuations, which bankrupt an increasing proportion of producers, can be avoided only if the producers organize into associations and set targets that are not to be exceeded for each type of produce. This is called the organization of markets and is, in fact, an example of corporatist self-organization.

I cannot see why a complex society should not seek to co-ordinate all these sectoral plans, both private and public, and to define medium- and long-term priorities, orientations and goals for the whole of the economy. What I am talking about, in short, is a "framework plan". In reality, the question is not whether there should be planning or not, but who plans and in whose interest they plan.

The economic failure of the countries of Central and Eastern Europe was due not to the principle of planning but to the conditions and the methods employed. These prevented enterprises not only from competing but from even knowing what their costs were, and were thus an obstacle to the adoption of economically rational behaviour. Moreover, instead of reining in the operation of the economy to make it serve society, they forced society to serve the creation of an economic apparatus. The result was a non-society and a non-economy – the very opposite of socialism.

Yet the point is that it is quite possible to plan and socially control the adjustment of supply and demand without suppressing either competition between enterprises or the knowledge of costs.

Keane: The emphasis you place on the reduction of working hours may seem surprising when we look more closely at the transformations that technological changes have brought about in working conditions and labour relations. Weren't the allergic reaction to work and the refusal of work, which were very widespread in the early 1970s, due to the repetitive character of jobs in the Taylorized factory or office? Isn't capitalist production increasingly using what Sabel and Piore call "flexible specialization" in highly computerised production units in which the old semi-skilled workers have given way to teams of multi-skilled operators who are highly trained, enjoy a great degree of autonomy, and are more like craft workers than old-style semi-skilled workers? Don't you underestimate the reskilling of workers, the rebirth of genuine craft work as a result of computerization?

Gorz: There have always been two tendencies within the labour movement: the glorification of work and the aspiration to work less. Those who glorified work were, for the most part, skilled workers who wielded great technical power within the factories. It seemed to them that it ought to be possible to transform that power into political power: they thought the workers should collectively appropriate the means of production, become the dominant class, and make the economy function for the benefit of all. The glorification of labour was therefore also a way of highlighting the strength of the working class. The more the workers identified with their role in production, the more they cast doubt on the solidity and legitimacy of the bourgeoisie's power. Their work was the source of all wealth; the economy was based on industries and crafts with workers as numerous as soldiers in a great army: miners, steelworkers, boilermakers, navvies, and so on.

But all that has completely changed. Identification with work and the glorification of work can no longer have the sense of an identification with the working class and a glorification of its might. This is a fact that certain sociologists – particularly sociologists of industrial labour relations – will not see. Whether consciously or not, they want to preserve within their analyses the idea of a working class that derives from its technical power an aspiration to exercise political power and take control of the means of production.

We must first of all situate the new multiskilled professional workers, who are autonomous in their work, in their context: labour is no longer the main productive force, and the length of working time is no longer the measure of wealth. Enterprises are replacing human work by computer-integrated automatic systems, which produce more, better and more flexibly with a smaller and smaller fraction of the workforce previously required. Semi-skilled workers and labourers are increasingly being eliminated from industry, but so are the traditional craft workers in the metalworking industries, such as toolmakers, millers and fitters. Machine tools controlled by microprocessors and flexible manufacturing systems no longer require those skills. Industry needs people who are capable of independent teamwork, and of co-ordinating their initiatives and skills without having anyone to supervise them or give them orders. They have to take responsibility for a complex system of machines and robots which, above all, require maintenance and immediate repair whenever there is the slightest breakdown. These new skilled workers have to be committed to their work. They have to be able to adapt to rapidly changing techniques and to acquire new skills, both manual and intellectual. For doing so, the enterprise offers them a privileged status and salary.

Keane: This trend is sometimes seen as a sign of the renewal of working-class attempts to achieve liberation, or at least achieve control over production.

Gorz: That is laughable, because the basic question is this: What fraction of the working class acquires these skills and this status? Today, less than

10 per cent. Tomorrow that stratum of "modern expert workers", as Kern and Schumann call them, will come to represent 25 per cent of the workers in industry, and perhaps even 40 per cent in the metalworking industries, we are told. That's fine, but what will become of the other 75 or 60 per cent? What will they end up as? We know the answer already: they will become "peripheral workers", condemned, as in years gone by, to perform the thankless unskilled tasks, with no possibility of career advancement. For the most part, they will become temporary workers, with a precarious status, who can be taken on and laid off again according to the needs of the moment.

But there is more. Peripheral workers and privileged new skilled workers make up a workforce that is constantly declining. In the long term, industry is tending to employ fewer and fewer people. The question, therefore, is not merely what fraction of the working class do the new privileged skilled workers represent? but also what fraction of the working population does the working class represent? What do the others do, those who have been eliminated – how nice it would be to say "liberated" – from industrial work? How do they live? How much do they earn?

If work and involvement in industry are to have some meaning, it is impossible not to ask these questions. And if you ask them, it is impossible to rest content with the improvement of the conditions of one group of workers in one sector of industry, unless you are willing to see the new work elite become a corporatist, conservative stratum, caring only for the defence of its privileges. It is impossible to take the existence of this elite as a pretext for glorifying work – all work – since it is precisely the work of this stratum that explains why jobs – full-time, permanent jobs – are no longer available for the unemployed and for workers in precarious employment. To glorify the work of an industrial elite when there aren't enough jobs to go around is no longer to glorify the strength of the working class, but rather to induce that elite to see itself as distinct from the working class, and to break its ties of solidarity with it. And in fact this is what employers' propaganda is doing.

Keane: Overall, you are saying that technical change is destroying the working class. It is the working class that is disintegrating, not capitalism. You don't, then, believe any more in the possible unity of the working class and its central importance to any strategy for transforming society?

Gorz: That's not what I'm saying. The front of labour – of trade-union struggle – remains crucial, but there is no central front any more. Society won't be changed without a trade-union movement worthy of the name "movement", but the creative impulses most often come from elsewhere. The central conflict is located at a level much deeper than labour disputes. The worker elite is indeed a participant in this central conflict. I am not by any means saying that it is a corporatist and conservative stratum. I am saying only that we push it in that direction when we constantly invoke the work ethic and the ideology of productivism in a way that redounds to its credit. This is what Mrs Thatcher did for ten years, with telling results. The task of the trade-union movement and trade-union policy is to open up a different path and other horizons for that elite. Instead of simply telling it that it is doing exciting work with which we can identify, we also have to tell it, in my opinion, that its work leads to there being less and less work for the rest of us. And that you can't seriously do work that leads to the elimination of work and at the same time exalt work as the essential source of each person's identity. For the new industrial skilled workers, identifying with their occupation can't mean identifying with their job within a flexible manufacturing system while remaining deaf and blind to everything else. Identifying with their occupation means understanding it as a social skill, to be exercised in a responsible way. In other words, it means stepping back from the function they perform in production and asking themselves what social, economic and cultural ends it serves. In particular, it means considering the redistribution of work and the reduction of working hours as essential questions of the highest priority. It is, therefore, viewing work in the proper perspective, not identifying with it, that can lay the ground for trade-union power and unity. This is a basic difference from the traditional views of the working class and trade unionism.

Keane: Ten years ago, you called those who didn't identify with their work the "non-class of non-workers". You accorded them a crucial role in challenging capitalism. You were severely criticized for that view. How, in fact, can that movement ever become a co-ordinated social movement capable of sustained action to transform society? Moreover, hasn't mounting unemployment caused the allergy to wage labour, the non-identification with it, to disappear and be replaced by a frantic search for paid jobs of any kind?

Gorz: What I called the "non-class of non-workers" wasn't an identifiable and organizable stratum but the emergence of a thoroughgoing cultural change, which has continued to gain ground ever since: individuals no longer identify with their work, even when it is interesting and skilled, because it usually appears to them as a functional specialization in the service of a megamachine on which they have no hold. They no longer identify with their place in the social process of production, nor do they derive from it the sense of belonging to a class. The social order has disintegrated; neither in their occupational role, nor in family structures, nor in the spatial structuring of their surroundings can individuals find what the sociologists used to call a determinate "identity", a reassuring social image of what they are. They are thrown back on themselves, and have to search for and develop themselves in ways that are not given in advance. Paid work is at best one dimension among others of that quest; it is seldom the most important.

These themes have been variously developed since then. The Italian metalworkers' union, Fiom-CGIL, concluded in a quite recent report:

> we are engaged in a process of social change as a result of which work now occupies only a minor place in people's lives. More precisely, work – paid work – is losing its central position ... Work is valued only when it has the quality of autonomous creative activity. Otherwise it is regarded merely as a way of earning a living.

In their most recent writings, Franz Steinkühler, the leader of the German metalworkers' union in Frankfurt, and Bruno Trentin, secretary-general of the CGIL, state in almost identical terms that trade-union policy must consist in creating the social conditions that enable all individuals to realize their potential and fulfil themselves in activities of their own choice, whether paid or unpaid, and to choose their way of life and their working hours – within the framework, of course, of negotiated agreements.

This distancing from work is in no way confined to unskilled employees. Even among the most highly skilled, the capacity for autonomy and initiative exceeds the degree of autonomy allowed or demanded by the functional specialization of work, however complex and responsible this work may be. Unlike the traditional labour movement, people are challenging the system not as agents of produc-tion but as people who cannot identify with their work and are not satisfied by it. As citizens, residents of a particular area, users of a public service, members of an association, or parents, they see their paid work in a wider context and conclude that their skills could be better employed, that industry could use less polluting and less energy-consuming technologies, that their quality of life could be improved if the requirements of economic rationality were subordinated to those of ecology, if production decisions were not made to get the best possible return on the largest possible amount of capital.

You have, then, a multidimensional social movement that can no longer be defined in terms of class antagonisms, and in which people's aim is to reappropriate an environment that the megatools have alienated from them, to regain control of their lives by reappropriating the skills that have been taken from them by the expertocracies on which big business and big government base their domination. This movement is essentially a struggle for collective and individual rights to self-determination, integrity, individual sovereignty. That struggle concerns all the different strata of wage-earners. It is fought in many different fields, and the company level is not always and not necessarily the most important of these. That's why the trade-union movement has a future only if it expands beyond the workplace and equips itself with what Bruno Trentin calls "structures of movement", public forums accessible to all, and opens itself up to debate, to common action, to alliance with other movements.

Keane: All in all, then, you are advocating political coalitions, new solidarities, and new alliances: between wage-earners in stable employment and the unemployed and precariously employed; between movements and parties. But do you believe that attempts to forge these solidarities and alliances can succeed?

Gorz: The question doesn't arise in precisely these terms. It isn't a matter of building coalitions or alliances between specific or sectoral interests – between elite workers and the unemployed and precarious workers, for example – but of winning new freedoms, new rights, which are by nature universal. People who set out to win or defend rights don't form either coalitions or alliances: they strive for what seems to them to be the common good, and that is what gives the movement its unity. This is the case with the women's movement, the anti-racist movement, and the movement for a healthy environment. The battle for a reduction in working hours can be understood in this same way: as a struggle for a set of rights and freedoms, which may obviously assume highly differentiated forms, but whose contents are the same for everybody – the right to learn, to study at any age (not simply to "retrain"), to bring up one's children, to engage in political or public activities, to stay at home with a sick or dying relative or friend, and so forth. These rights to what Marx calls "the free development of individuality" presuppose having not only the available time but also the right to the self-management of one's time within relatively flexible limits.

No insurmountable difficulties are raised, therefore, by the idea of bringing together all the different strata of wage-earners in solidarity, provided that the campaign for reducing working hours takes into account the diversity of situations involved. A reduction in weekly working hours isn't necessarily in everyone's interest. It may best suit those with stable employment, since their jobs require regular and continuous presence at the workplace. For a large number of skilled personnel, however, a linear reduction of the working day and the working week is not a possibility, particularly in the case of computer programmers, designers, technicians involved in setting up and testing new installations, and so on. A reduction in annual working hours in the form of weeks or months of extra leave, together with entitlement to sabbatical years, will be more appropriate for people in these occupations, since their work requires imagination, ideas, and the refreshing of multidisciplinary knowledge, all of which are less easily acquired at the workplace than in discussion, reading, travel, stepping back from the tasks of the moment and varying one's activities and interests. The idea that the specialist can keep abreast of things only by total devotion to his or her specialism bears no relation to reality. It merely serves the interests of a system of domination that seeks to imprison people in their specialist fields in order to prevent them from questioning, as citizens, the ends that the decision-makers are making them serve.

Lastly, there is that 40 to 50 per cent of the working population for whom the economy offers only casual, temporary, part-time employment: the unemployed and the precarious workers. The shrinking of the volume of work needed by the economy, which could be a source of freedom if it were distributed to all, is imposed as a deprivation on this fraction of the working population. These people, who can be hired and fired at will, are paid only for the work they do, not for their availability and capacity to work during the periods of forced unemployment. If we examine their situation closely, we see that they are victims of a discrimination whose rationale is essentially ideological. They are used as an example to show that only time actually worked entitles a person to remuneration and, therefore, that working time must remain the measure of wealth and social usefulness. Now, these basic principles of capitalist ideology are, in fact, breached where the majority of workers in stable employment are concerned. Maintenance technicians, operators and controllers of automated plants, medical personnel, and workers in emergency services are paid for their availability and their capacity to intervene, not for work actually done. The ideology of maximum efficiency and of basing wages on the measurement of output is rendered obsolete by technological development. The case of the unemployed and precarious workers allows it to preserve a semblance of existence.

That is why a French group, the Association of the Unemployed and Precarious Workers, is demanding, in a wholly plausible and legitimate way, that people employed on a precarious basis as temporary or casual workers should be given the right, during periods when wage-labour is interrupted, to an income that remunerates them for remaining available for work. In exchange, they commit themselves to performing a certain annual amount of work, if it so happens that they are offered any. This is equivalent, in fact, to calling for a reduction in the working year and for the right to work intermittently without any substantial reduction of income. The discontinuous nature of the wage relation is to be transformed into a new freedom instead of being suffered as a constraint imposed by management. There is nothing strange about such a demand. Until the 1910s, it was abnormal for a worker – particularly a good craft worker – to work in a stable job the whole year long. For those workers, frequent job changes, unemployment, travelling, and casual work were all ways of preserving their independence both from management and from wage-labour. That taste for change, for independence and autonomy, reappeared some time ago among a proportion of the workforce that is too large to be dismissed as insignificant. These workers, most of them young, prefer temporary work to stable, full-time employment, as this leaves them free to engage in activities that are more fulfilling than most of those by which one can earn a living.

Keane: This distancing from work no doubt has its positive side. But it is important to point out that in the OECD countries, between 70 and 90 per cent of part-time workers, most of whom are in precarious forms of employment, are women between twenty-five and forty-four years old, employed in the service sector. For many of these women, working shortened hours means working a "double shift": unpaid work at home plus paid work – generally poorly paid – with no chance of career advancement. The result is that a great many women have much less free time and are more overworked than men.

Gorz: Quite so. It's doubly iniquitous and doubly scandalous.

In the first place, the economic system produces increasing wealth with a decreasing quantity of work. Yet it refuses to redistribute the work in such a way that everyone can work less and better without loss of income. It prefers to have a section of the population working full-time, another section unemployed, and a third, which is constantly growing in numbers, working a shortened day for reduced pay.

Furthermore, most full-time jobs are held by men and most jobs with reduced working hours by women. That is another scandal, which we shall be rid of only when paid working hours are reduced for everyone. If the normal working week were no more than thirty hours – which is the target of the Left and of trade unions in the Netherlands, Italy and Germany – then the present sexual division of labour would lose its economic foundation, and there would be no way to excuse it.

This is certainly the trend. First, an increasing proportion of young fathers are requesting shorter working hours or leave – even unpaid leave – in order to be able to look after their children. Four years ago, the figure was 12 per cent in the United States. A year ago it was 26 per cent, and half of American firms offer their male employees the option of working shorter hours. Second, almost half of French, German and Swiss couples stay unmarried, and in half of these cases they don't live together. The children live with the mother, with the father, or with each in turn. This fundamentally changes the meaning of unpaid domestic labour. Women or men who live alone do their housework for themselves, not for the greater profit or comfort of their partner. So as this trend continues, there is no longer any sense in asking society to recognize the social usefulness of household labour by paying wages for housework. However, this development lends a greater urgency and enhanced legitimacy to the demand for the right to paid parental leave, a sabbatical year, or other forms of reducing time at work.

This kind of right is often claimed on behalf of the "social usefulness" of the mother's (or father's) work in the home. The argument is that the social value of housework must be recognized as equal to the value of paid work. I don't agree with that approach, which takes as its basic criterion the individual's usefulness to society, because it implicitly denies the autonomy of the individual and the existence of his or her inalienable rights *upon* society. We must abandon the idea that society has priority and that individuals make themselves useful by reproducing it, and instead reverse the terms. Society will be better in so far as it acknowledges the rights of individuals to fulfil themselves, and grants them the opportunities for such fulfilment. The right to motherhood, to fatherhood, to take care of one's body and one's habitat, to "look after oneself" and look after one's neighbour, must be unconditional and privileged. It is on this basis that society will be created.

Keane: Isn't the extension of free time also a means of reducing overconsumption? The more commodities we consume, the more we need to work to buy them and the less time we have for other activities, including the activity of being citizens.

Gorz: Yes, and the opposite is true too: the more you work, the more you tend to consume commodities, but also to consume commodity services, since you don't have the time or energy to do things by and for yourself. The obligation to work full-time has been the key to economic growth in the affluent capitalist societies. The Swedish economist Gunnar Adler-Karlson was, I think, the first to say this in his book *The Unimportance of Full Employment.* If we could adjust our working time to the needs we really feel, how many hours would we work? But this possibility of "choosing our working hours" isn't offered to us. It would enable us to limit our consumption of commodities, which has become an ecological imperative in the affluent nations. And the possibility of choosing our working hours will be all the greater a the normal weekly or annual working hours become shorter.

Keane: In *Ecology as Politics*, you adopt two contradictory points of view. On the one hand you say that the ecological approach is incompatible with capitalist rationality; on the other you argue that capitalism will eventually accept ecological imperatives, just as it eventually accepted universal suffrage and the forty-hour week. Thus, according to you, these imperatives mustn't be ends in themselves for the Green movement. Why this ambiguity?

Gorz: The ecological movement can't be reduced to the demand that the environment be protected. If it is, its demands will end up sooner or later being taken on board by capitalism – and nothing will change. We shall have – we already have – eco-business and an eco-industry, and we could have a techno-ecosphere, if not indeed techno-ecofascism as described in science fiction. Capitalism may develop a highly profitable eco-business, just as it developed a highly profitable arms industry, to meet public contracts. And in response to new pollution standards, it may better eliminate and recycle industrial waste products and adopt different, more capital-intensive technologies, at the cost of higher prices and increased inequalities. This is the direction in which we are going at the moment: the growing pauperization of the poor and the increasing affluence of the well-off.

Unlike what is called "environmentalism" in the Anglo-Saxon countries, political ecology does not confine itself to trying to reduce the impact of the existing system of production on the environment. It challenges the reasons behind the development of a certain number of technologies, products, and forms of consumption in the first place. These reasons are contained in the logic of capitalist accumulation: it has to be possible for increasing quantities of capital to be invested at a profit, and this requires the consumption of an increasing flow of commodities and commodity services. The population, therefore, has to be induced to satisfy its needs through a maximum of consumption, and a maximum number of needs for commodity consumption have to be created. Now, many needs could be satisfied by a less intense flow of better, more durable products, and consumer needs themselves could be reduced by a more relaxed and convivial style of life that left more free time. We could live and work better by consuming less, provided that we consumed differently. It would not then be possible for technologies, social relations, our model of consumption, or our relation to nature to remain the same.

The "environmentalist" and "ecological" approaches are therefore fundamentally different from each other. The former imposes new constraints and new limitations on the free operation of economic rationality as developed by capitalism. But these constraints and limitations don't alter the basic tendency of the system, which is to extend the sphere of economic rationality and increase the value of rising amounts of capital. The ecological approach, in contrast, involves a paradigm shift, which may be summarized in the slogan "less but better". It aims to reduce the sphere in which economic rationality and commodity exchanges apply, and to subordinate it to non-quantifiable societal and cultural ends and to the free development of individuals. The ecological restructuring of the economy envisaged within the Left in Germany and the Netherlands and within the Italian extreme Left thus necessarily has an anti-capitalist, socialist direction to it. Investment can no longer have economic growth as its goal, but only negative growth and an accompanying expansion of those activities not governed by monetary evaluation and the pursuit of maximum efficiency and profit.

Keane: The German "Greens" were the first to popularize the idea of a guaranteed social income, or "universal grant". This idea is now making headway all over Europe, particularly in the Netherlands, where it is supported by all the Left movements, by some of the trade unions, and by many influential personalities. It is being debated in Italy, and it has given rise in France to the creation of the "minimum insertion income". A guaranteed social income for everyone is regarded by many as a citizen's right – the right to a "citizenship wage". It could also be the most important way of redistributing paid work fairly and reducing the length of working hours. Now, you have come out against such a formula on several occasions. You would rather have a system that guarantees every citizen a normal wage throughout his or her lifetime in exchange for performing over that lifetime a quantity of work, which would decrease and become more and more intermittent as social productivity increased. It is often held against you that by linking the right to an income with the right to work, you are crucially linking the right to an income with an obligation to work. Isn't there a contradiction between an obligation of this kind and the break with the ideology of work that you advocate elsewhere?

Gorz: I consider utopian, in the bad sense of the term, ideal objectives that don't indicate new possibilities for emancipatory action. This is the critique I would make, as Jürgen Habermas does, of Hannah Arendt's disciples, who see the "citizenship wage" as a way to revive the ideal of the Greek polis. I see two fundamental defects in this universal-allowance idea.

The first is that an allowance of this kind, in exempting people from performing any paid work, fails to create a public space for non-economic activities. Economic activity today occupies the public space to an exaggerated extent, and Arendt was right to wish to press it back, allowing more scope for political activities, activities that concern the "common good". It will not, however, be ousted from that space by paying an allowance to those who stay outside the economic sphere, and thereby remain outside what is today the most important dimension of the public sphere. On the contrary, an allowance that exempts people from any work within the economic sphere will deepen the split within society. Economic activity will become the province of production-mad, profit-hungry individuals. They will tend to monopolize the public space and marginalize the non-working recipients of state allowances, who will then be condemned to a life of private activities and social oblivion. If you want other activities to supplant work within the public space, then the importance of work has to be reduced through organized public action, which simultaneously opens up the public space to activities whose ends are not economic, and helps to establish such activities in that space. That is why, in my opinion, we have to come at the problem "from below", by reducing the number of working hours. And this has to be conceived not as a single measure but as a long-term, general policy, concerning both government and trade unions, and embodying an alternative view of civilization. Trade-union action – action by trade unions with a much broader conception of their role and, as argued by Negt in Germany and Trentin in Italy, a different structure – is indispensable if that objective is to be achieved. This is true, first, because only the (renovated) trade union can organize the population in the public space of work and open up that space to public activities outside the workplace; and second, because the shortening of working hours has to be worked out in concrete detail, and applied through collective action and bargaining at all levels. A new "contract for society" has to be established so that social relations can be transformed. A universal allowance created by a law and paid out by an administrative agency would not have the same scope.

The right to work has to be understood in this context – as a *political* right of access to what is currently the chief activity within the public sphere and to the powers that access confers, in particular the power to participate in decisions relating to the organization of economic activity and its place in society. It is quite conceivable, of course, that the unemployed should take part, by rights, with their own associations, in the formulation of trade-union policy. But unemployment then has to be understood as a temporary and partial interruption of participation in economic activity, not as a choice not to participate in it at all. By opening up this right to non-participation, the universal-grant idea in fact creates two categories of citizen, and gives society the right to perpetuate forms of social exclusion.

The second defect of the universal grant can be seen if we approach the problem from the opposite angle. A certain quantity of work is essential for the existence of society and social individuals. That necessity is imposed by the nature of things, not by a social obligation. In the ancient polis, economically necessary work was confined to the private sphere and reserved for women and slaves. The private sphere was the sphere of authoritarian constraint, whereas the public sphere was the sphere of free citizens, of men freed from the burden of necessity. The emancipation of the slaves reversed this type of political order. The equality and freedom of individuals now requires that necessary work be socially organized in the public sphere, where everyone participates. No one must bear the burden of necessity for the benefit of others, and no one, therefore, must be exempted from bearing his or her share of that burden. Now, the universal-grant idea opens up the right to exemption. It allows society not to concern itself with distributing the burden equitably. In so doing, out of idealism, it plays along with the ideology of work: it seems to consider work as an elective, optional activity, which can be reserved for those who like doing it. But the point is that work has to be done, whether we like it or not, and it is only by starting out from the recognition of its necessity that we can try to make it as pleasant and fulfilling as possible, to lessen its intensity and shorten its duration.

Admittedly, not all necessary work can be organized socially in the public sphere, nor should it be. There is a sphere within which individuals must belong to themselves and sovereignly produce themselves, free from all control and from social norms. This is the private sphere. Necessary work within that sphere cannot have the same status as work in the public sphere. I call this "work-for-oneself". It is ambivalent, being at once burdensome and gratifying, or each of these in turn, depending on the circumstances. Not doing such work means entrusting it to servants. It is mainly made up of all the various activities of self-maintenance. Such work will be less burdensome and more gratifying as free time is more abundant, on a daily, weekly and yearly basis.

Keane: If working time is gradually reduced to the point where paid work becomes intermittent, what will people live on during the intervals between work? You have spoken of a guaranteed social income spread out over a lifetime, to be paid in exchange for a decreasing amount of work. But employers, and even a large number of trade unions, will tell you that the cost of such a system would be beyond what the economy could bear.

Gorz: The six-day week and the eight-hour day were originally regarded as ruinous demands. The present social security system would have seemed completely unrealistic seventy years ago. At the beginning of the century, full-time employment meant working more than three thousand hours a year. In 1960, the figure was twenty-one hundred. In 1985, it was sixteen hundred hours, yet this volume of work, which was 25 per cent lower than the 1960 figure, produced a GNP two-and-a-half times higher. In his latest book, Jacques Delors points out that in 1946, a twenty-year-old wage-earner could expect to spend a third of his or her waking life at work. By 1975, this had fallen to a quarter, and today it is less than a fifth. He adds that this development will continue, and that it should "give rise to other logics of production and exchange". In fact, if you consider the different types of leave from work, whether paid or covered by insurance, full-time work is already i\termittent. There is no reason why we shouldn't gradually get back to an average of one thousand working hours a year – which was the norm in the eighteenth century – or twenty to thirty thousand hours a lifetime, enabling everyone successively to adopt several lifestyles, jobs, careers, or types of activity without ever ceasing to receive a full wage. We have to get used to thinking of free time as a major part of life, not as just the inferior time left over after work. It is the time in which paid work is done that has to become – and, in fact, already is – secondary in importance.

Keane: But if people are to be paid uninterruptedly for increasingly discontinuous work, what will force them to resume socially necessary activity after several months' or even one or two years' break? If people are actually to do the amount of work that entitles them to a guaranteed income during their lifetimes, won't a whole system of bureaucratic controls be needed? Won't people have to possess a logbook, as they did in Czechoslovakia, for example, recording the exact amount of work they have performed?

Gorz: Your pension fund already contains a record of the number of weeks and months you have worked and what you have earned over your lifetime. Instead of being paid from the age of fifty-five – or even fifty – onwards for a period of complete inactivity that will continue until you die, why shouldn't you be entitled to spread that out economically – but not socially – inactive period over your life? It is no more difficult to manage by computer. A number of points is allocated for each working period, and these entitle you to a certain period of leave, paid on the basis of the average of what you have earned in your previous jobs. If you go too long without working, the computer sends you a letter warning you that you have only three months, say, to find work again. And the system could be combined with regulatory incentives. If, for some reason or other, there is a sudden need for nursing staff or bricklayers, the right to leave could be suspended and those on leave encouraged to work; they might, for example, be offered a higher number of points for going back to work. The Swedish economist Gösta Rehn was the first to propose a system of this kind, with incentives added, allowing people to take a kind of advance on their retirement at any age. One can imagine half a dozen other schemes, and raise objections to each of them. I am not defending any particular system, but I am saying there is a need to imagine a way out of the "work-based society" towards a society in which activities performed for non-economic ends – whether public or private, social or personal – will be preponderant.

Keane: But these will still have to be financed, since you yourself do not believe in a society without money in which everything would be free. This presupposes fiscal and monetary policy.

Gorz: That policy must reconcile three types of interest that appear to be contradictory: first, the legitimate interest of people who don't want their real incomes to fall when their working hours are reduced; second, the legitimate interest of enterprises, whether public or private, which can be managed efficiently and with foresight only if they know their real costs and are not made to pay people they don't actually need; third, the legitimate interest of society, which has to be able to establish priorities and discourage certain forms of consumption and production by deterrent taxes similar to those that already exist, from which export products are exempt.

We have to conceive, then, a way of financing all this that does not burden either the incomes of working individuals or the manufacturing costs of enterprises. This is the case with taxes on consumption, of the VAT type, which could be very greatly increased on those industrial products whose relative prices are continually falling. These taxes would supply a fund that would pay people their incomes during non-working periods. But you could also envisage having different types of money – for example, a "circulation money" that couldn't be hoarded, a "neighbourhood money", for trading services, that could not circulate, and so forth. In short, "other logics of production and exchange", as Jacques Delors says.

A political strategy centred on the reduction of working hours may be the main lever with which we can shift the balance within society, and put an end to the domination of the political sphere by the economic. And this would mean the extinction of capitalism.

Keane: Perhaps not. It might also lead to a post-Keynesian era that would leave privately controlled capital a significant role, albeit reduced by comparison with the previous period. Aren't you supposing that capitalism can be destroyed by stealth, and that capitalists resemble old men on their deathbeds, ready to sign over their estates?

Gorz: I'm quite happy to accept what you call "a significant role, albeit reduced", for capital. That is precisely what is meant by the extinction of capital*ism*. We have to distinguish between capitalism and the logic of capital. Capitalism is a social system in which life, activities, the scale of values, and the aims of individuals and society are all dominated by relations subordinated to economic rationality and directed towards the valorization of capital. The logic of capital, by contrast, is the only form of pure economic rationality. There is no economically rational way to run an enterprise other than capitalist management. That is an obvious fact which everyone has come to acknowledge. But it doesn't mean that all enterprises and activities have to obey capitalist management, or that the pure economic rationality such management represents must, or even can, take priority over all other considerations, at the level either of the enterprise or of society as a whole. The criterion of economic efficiency demands the pursuit of the greatest possible productivity per unit of (dead or live) labour. In practice, this means the pursuit of maximum profit. But this criterion is applicable only to a restricted area of what Marx called our "exchanges with nature". The application of the criterion of measurable productivity has, then, to be restricted by the application of criteria of a totally different kind. When these criteria win out over the logic of capital in public decision-making and individual behaviour, and assign economic rationality the subordinate role of a means in the service of non-economic ends, then we shall have got beyond capitalism to a different society, if not indeed a different civilization.

Of course, you might object that the capitalists will resist fiercely, and their resistance will have to be overcome. How? By whom? This brings us back to the problem I mentioned a moment ago. There is a central conflict, but no central front; there are antagonisms similar to the class struggle, but no class capable of hegemony. Who got the better of the formidable political and financial power of the nuclear industry in Sweden, Austria, Switzerland, Germany, Italy? Who turned such things as the extinction of species, the destruction of the tropical rainforests, the hole in the ozone layer, global warming, the pollution of groundwater, industrial agriculture, and factory livestock farming into themes of a debate that confronts all political forces throughout Europe, and seems ready to lead not just to technocratic measures but to radical structural reforms?

There is a movement, a change; we're seeing transverse alliances that cut across class boundaries. Each of us knows some capitalist or other – a top manager in the chemical industry, for example – who is racked with doubt about what he is doing, and wonders what his deathbed assessment of his life's work will be, or what his great-grandchildren will think of him. Cultural change and ideas have a force of their own, even on people whose interests they upset. Admittedly, the managers of the capitalist megamachine won't be converted spontaneously to ecological self-limitation and socialist democracy. But quite a few of them will be relieved and even prepared to co-operate when public pressure and legislators ask them to serve goals more defensible than merely maximizing profit to the detriment of people's health and the quality of life.

Translated by Chris Turner in
collaboration with André Gorz

9

Shorter Hours, Same Pay[1]

Rising unemployment will not be prevented by emergency measures. Medium- and long-term policies, implemented both by the unions and by government, are required if everyone is to be entitled to socially useful work, to the development of their capacities, to a reduction in working hours without loss of earnings and to the increasing self-management of their time.

Such a policy is outlined in the following pages, which were originally written for French trade unionists who had argued at a seminar that working hours could not be reduced without loss of earnings if additional jobs were to be created as a result. "If paid work is distributed over a greater number of people," they said, "isn't it inevitable that each person's income will be lower?" We shall see that this need not be so. So as not to complicate matters needlessly, the first part of this chapter is confined to a macro-economic argument, but leaves aside the diminution of unit costs which, in capital-intensive companies, may result from a more extended use of existing machinery made possible by reduced working hours (RWH).

Working Hours, Pay and Employment

RWH is both desirable and necessary. It is desirable in so far as it gives each person more freedom in the way they organize their life, more freedom to engage in varied pursuits and thus to enrich their lives. It is necessary to the extent that advances in productivity make it possible to produce more with less work. If everyone is to be able to find work, the quantity of work performed by each person must progressively diminish. On this point there is a more or less general agreement.

As soon as we go beyond general principles, however, there is such confusion regarding ways and means that RWH, instead of bringing unity, creates division between the holders of steady jobs, on the one hand, and the unemployed or holders of casual or contingent jobs, on the other. All advocates of an RWH policy, including the Left alternative theorists, continue to assert that present levels of purchasing power could not be maintained if working hours were reduced. Such an assertion is understandable when it comes from members of the Green movement who stand apart by choice from the labour movement and the Left. For them, the aim must be to bring about *a negative growth* in industrial and commodity production for the benefit of "own-use" artisanal production and non-commodity exchange of services. They therefore declare themselves in favour of an RWH with a proportionate reduction in earnings. They do not say it would be impossible to earn as much as in the past when fewer hours are worked; they say it would not be desirable.

Among the immense majority of economists, by contrast, including those of the alternative Left, the maintenance of present levels of purchasing power is regarded as an economic impossibility. Alain Lipietz, for example, who is no advocate of zero growth (nor, *a fortiori*, of negative growth), estimates that compensatory payment for the hours cut could be made at only 70 per cent of the previous wage level, and that if one wishes to guarantee those workers who earn up to twice the statutory minimum wage the maintenance of their purchasing power, "this means a more drastic reduction for salaries exceeding 8,000 francs [£930] per month". This means that the RWH policy would very probably alienate the most educated and influential fraction of the active, employed population from the outset.

But by what reasoning do economists assert that purchasing power has to fall when working hours are reduced? The point is by no means scientifically proven. Do we not work half as many hours today as at the beginning of the century, and yet receive real incomes that are not half the size but five times bigger? Why, when sources of productivity gains are far from exhausted, could we not keep our current level of purchasing power in the future?

A number of trade unionists said to me recently, "All right, productivity gains can finance shorter working hours with no loss of income. But if you want to create extra jobs as well, so as to reduce unemployment, you'll have to reduce wages."

The fact is that they were wrong, as I shall demonstrate in a moment, unless we assume a situation of zero growth. Despite what they say, for as long as not only productivity but also output continue to grow – even slightly – it is possible to do everything at once: reduce working hours, bring about a fall in unemployment and maintain, or even increase, incomes.

If we find it so hard to admit this possibility – and to desire it – this is because we always reason *ex post*, as economists say – that is, starting out from a situation which is the final outcome of a *past* development. From this point of view, the die is already cast: the fruits of economic growth and productivity gains have always *already been shared out*. They cannot be distributed a second time, between a greater number of people, without reducing the share each person receives.

But what seems impossible retrospectively becomes possible if we reason *ex ante* on the best way to allocate the fruits of a development that is *yet to come*. The division of the spoils then becomes a matter of political decision as to how the future is to be shaped.

The questions we then face are the following: what productivity gains can we expect over the next four or five years? And what increases in output? How are they to be divided between (a) a reduction in working hours, (b) the creation of additional jobs, and (c) improving wages and social benefits?

In short, the point is to steer a process which is actually in progress by choosing the needs it is to serve. Either politics is the sum of such choices, or it is nothing.

Let us look at the range of political choices currently available to us. To begin with, I shall take the rates of economic growth and the productivity gains of these last few years as a base, projecting them forward over the next four years. I shall even underestimate them to a small degree, so as to be forearmed against possible random fluctuations and against the accusation of being unrealistic. Let us, therefore, forecast the following course of development.[*]

A. In four years, production will have increased by 8 per cent and productivity by 12 per cent

In other words, to produce 108 per cent of the current volume of disposable wealth, a quantity of labour of just 96 per cent will be needed (100+8−12).

Theoretically, we have four different options.

---

[*] *Translator's note*: The following calculations start out from the assumption of the standard French thirty-nine-hour week.

1. We maintain current working hours

The workforce will fall by 4 per cent to reach 96 per cent of the earlier level.

> Workforce: –4%

Direct and indirect wages may rise by about 12 per cent, i.e. by as much as disposable wealth (8 per cent) spread over 96 per cent of the previous workforce.

> Wages: +12%

This is roughly what has happened in industry during the recent period.

2. We maintain employment at current levels

Since they produce 8 per cent more in 4 per cent fewer hours of work, wages may increase by 8 per cent for a level of work reduced by 4 per cent. This is what has happened in some public services and "advanced" enterprises.

> Wages: +8%
> Working hours: –4%

3. We maintain wages at current levels

We can then (theoretically) employ 8 per cent more workers, as there will be 8 per cent more to distribute; and we can reduce working hours by 12 per cent (to 34 hours a week), as there will be 8 per cent more people to do 4 per cent less work.

> Workforce: +8%
> Working hours: –12%

4. We reduce working hours while increasing wages and the workforce

We could, for example, employ 5 per cent more workers, increase wages on average by 3 per cent and reduce working hours by 9 per cent (to 35½ hours per week). If we employ 6 per cent more people, working hours can be reduced by 10 per cent (to a 35-hour week) and wages increased by 2 per cent.

Workforce:	+5%
Wages:	+3%
Working hours:	–9%

There is no real need to examine a fifth scenario in which wages are reduced, since even with wages held constant, the workforce should increase by 8 per cent (1.8 million people in four years). In a complex, developed economy, it is practically impossible to do much better than this, unless one creates a lot of unskilled and petty jobs, which is not the objective.

It is worth pointing out in passing, however, that if productivity and output increase at the same rate of 12 per cent in four years, wages could increase by 4 per cent and the workforce by 8 per cent for working hours that are reduced by 8 per cent (to a 36-hour week). This, however, is a hypothesis which we would do better not to envisage. Sustained growth in the volume of production is incompatible with the ecological restructuring that is now on the agenda in all the industrialized countries, where the link between producing more and living better has been broken.

In order to live better, we now have to produce and consume differently, to do better and more with less, by eliminating sources of waste to begin with (for example, unnecessary packaging, poor heat insulation, the predominance of road transport) and by increasing product durability.

B. Let us suppose, then, that as a result of its efforts to eliminate waste, extend the life of products, change agricultural methods and reduce the causes of accidents and illness, ecological restructuring had the effect of halting economic growth. Let us also suppose that productivity does not rise by more than 9 per cent in four years. How will zero growth modify the options that remain open? In this case, there will only be three possibilities:

1. We maintain current working hours

The workforce falls by 9 per cent in this case, since the same level of output requires 9 per cent less work, and those who retain their jobs can earn 9 per cent more. It's just bad luck for the others.

2. We maintain the workforce at the current level

Since we can produce as much with 9 per cent less work, working hours can be reduced by 9 per cent (to approximately 35 hours per week) without any cut in wages.

3. We reduce working hours while increasing the workforce by 4 per cent

There will then be 4 per cent more of us to achieve a level of output which requires 9 per cent less work. Working hours can therefore be reduced by about 13 per cent (34 hours a week). But wages will have to be reduced by 4 per cent as the same volume of wealth has to be shared out among 4 per cent more workers.

It must be emphasized here that wages do not have to be reduced *in proportion* to the reduction in working hours: for working hours set at 87 per cent of the previous level, wages will be 96 per cent of what they were before. This corresponds to the hypothesis advanced by Alain Lipietz of paying compensation for the hours that have been cut at 70 per cent of the previous wage level. But *this hypothesis applies only if there is zero growth.* That is why the question arises: should we opt, from the outset, for zero (or even negative) growth, as the ecologists think?

The answer to this question will determine the system of alliances on which a policy of ecological restructuring can be based, and its chances of being accepted socially. Choosing zero growth means, in fact, that a third of all job-holders – those at the top of the scale – who are also the most influential politically and culturally will have to accept reductions in their purchasing power. These reductions will not easily be accepted, since it will be necessary not only to maintain or even improve the real incomes of the workers at the bottom of the scale but also to raise the general level of skills and qualifications, and increase the proportion of highly skilled jobs. It is, in fact, these latter that will have to grow most rapidly in the wake of a substantial RWH. Can we increase the number of skilled jobs and, at the same time, reduce the levels of remuneration for such jobs? Can we expect the most skilled workers alone to suffer the drawbacks of a policy of RWH *before they have even been able to discover its advantages?*

I do not believe so. If we want the "strong" to show solidarity with the "weak", and if we want the RWH to respond to the interests and meet the aspirations of both the working elites and the unemployed or casually employed, then it is better, *in the initial stages,* for the economy to continue to grow a little, as it has continued to do, so as to be able both to cut back on unemployment and increase wages while reducing working hours (see scenario A 4). Everything will become easier thereafter, in the second four-year period, with the coming of the thirty-two-hour week, the elimination of most of the residual unemployment and the acceleration of a process of ecological restructuring enabling us to live better while consuming, producing and working less, but better.

BEYOND ECONOMICS

Society must aim today not to produce the greatest possible wealth but to enable everyone to engage in productive and disinterested activities which ensure their place in society and their personal development . . .

If the government were to acknowledge that wage-based society was running out of steam, it would have to recognize its responsibility for developing these disinterested activities. Work-sharing will be the more willingly accepted if everyone can engage in projects of personal development outside their work. The more attractive these disinterested activity projects are, the readier people will be to accept stable wages or only a slight progression in incomes.

GUY ROUSTANG, *L'emploi: un choix de société*,
Paris 1987.

How is a General RWH to be Financed?

Up until now, I have only demonstrated the theoretical possibility, on the macro-economic level, of a generalized reduction in working hours and unemployment, without loss of income. But this is in no way to confront the problem of implementing such a policy in the different branches of industry and enterprises. Reductions in working hours certainly cannot be made dependent on productivity gains achieved at enterprise or branch level. Such a policy would result in a twenty-eight-hour week for workers in the banking sector, while hospital staff would be working fifty-six hours for the same wage. The tendency for wages and working conditions to equalize out cannot be resisted. When it is not produced by the workings of the job market, such an equalization is, in the end, imposed by social struggles. Thus, to plan for a general reduction in working hours, equal for all, is both to obey the dictates of realism and to act with a sense of fairness. I will add immediately that *an RWH equal for all in no way prevents, but actually facilitates a policy of "free choice of working hours"* – that is, the adoption of individual patterns of working hours spread over the day, week, month or year.

Yet how are we to proceed so that an RWH equal for all – for example, 12 per cent in four years' time – really produces a situation in which a greater proportion of the active population can share in the fruits of productivity and growth? An RWH of 12 per cent will not, in fact, prevent shrinkages of the workforce in the branches (metalworking, chemicals, banks, postal services, railways, etc.) where productivity is increasing at a much quicker rate. By contrast, in the activities where productivity is increasing more slowly, the recruitment of additional staff has little chance of occurring spontaneously and in the arithmetically predictable quantities. There are several reasons for this.

First of all, the type of skill in the branches which are laying off labour does not immediately match the needs in the branches where productivity is stagnant. Second, when the normal working hours diminish by 12 per cent, for example, the workforces in these industries would have to increase by approximately 14 per cent (for the sake of simplicity I leave out of account productivity gains due to RWH itself); wage costs would therefore increase proportionately, and in many cases would, in the end, become prohibitive. Repair and maintenance services, for example, would continue to disappear: instead of having things repaired, they would be thrown away, except where they were designed to be repaired easily. On the other hand, the hotel and catering services and health and personal care would carry on becoming more concentrated and splitting into two groups: a "hand-made" sector offering personalized services to a small client-base which can afford its high rates, and an "off-the-peg", industrialized sector offering standardized, low-quality services to all-comers.

The development of this second category of services does, admittedly, create jobs, but it is a *net* creator of jobs only to the extent that, thanks to the drop in the relative price of services, it succeeds in reaching a new client-base. This fall in relative prices is itself possible only by virtue of an industrial rationalization of work which transforms artisanal activities into jobs with high productivity, but low skills and low wages. This is what has happened in the United States. The contraction in the number of stable jobs, paid at a rate equal to or higher than the median wage, has been accompanied by the rise in casual activities, paid at a rate far below the median wage and often below the legal minimum. Almost half of the American labour force are in precarious, part-time jobs of this kind, and do not work all the year round. Society has split into two almost equal parts.

The options here are clear. If we wish to reduce unemployment, as in the USA, by creating a great number of jobs in the commodity service sector, we have to accept the "dual society" in which a growing part of the population will perform underpaid and underskilled work, most often in the service of members of the workforce who still have steady, full-time jobs in the productive sector. Conversely, if we wish to avoid the "dual society", then, as Guy Roustang has so convincingly shown,[2] we cannot at the same time seek to solve the problem of unemployment by increasing the number of jobs in personal services. If these jobs are skilled, paid at normal rates and assured of the same social safeguards as work in the rest of the economy, their number will necessarily be more limited than it is in the USA or Japan, or even in Sweden.

To opt for a policy of RWH thus means opting against both the "dual society" and the endless proliferation of service jobs, since if these jobs are to have the same reductions in working hours and the same social safeguards as jobs in industry, they will inevitably become more expensive, and this will put a brake on their proliferation. This should not be seen as something negative, since *RWH has meaning only if, by virtue of the time it sets free, it enables people, households and communities to engage in activities which do not have remuneration as their purpose; and among these activities there will naturally be a place, among others, for those which increase each person or community's control over its own immediate environment, its own existence, its own desires and aspirations, its own fulfilment.* The desire *to be taken under the wing* of professionals or institutions diminishes as the cultural level and standard of living rise and the proportion of time each person has at their own disposal increases. It is supplanted by the desire for personal sovereignty, which expresses itself notably in contesting the hold which professionals, manufacturers, technologies and institutions seek to maintain over people by programming their behaviour, needs, tastes, plans and leisure. In a civilization based on disposable time, where working hours average thirty per week or less (i.e. approximately 1,100 hours per year), the importance of services whose function is to *save time* or to compensate for the lack of time *must* decline, giving way to activities whose aim is to *spend time* taking pleasure in what one is doing and giving, rather than in what one is consuming and receiving.

A policy of RWH objectively promotes a greater autonomy on the part of individuals; it must work consciously towards this, and not programme leisure in such a way as to colonize for the benefit of commodity consumption the time that has been set free. A policy of RWH implies that paid work is performed in the main by skilled persons who are well-paid, productive in the economic sense, and socially useful; it therefore implies that servant work, the aim of which is simply to do for others what they could have done just as well in the same time, does not expand.

A policy of RWH, therefore, will necessarily be selective in the types of services whose development it promotes. In particular, it will distinguish between cultural services in the broad sense – which tend towards the blossoming of personal capacities and of people's ability to take charge of their own lives, existential problems, health, and so on – and services essentially performed for profit, which tend to increase commodity consumption and dependency.

A selectiveness of this kind in the development of the service sector may be achieved through the way in which the RWH is financed. There can be no question of all enterprises increasing the hourly wage of their workers to preserve (at least) their purchasing power when working hours are shortened. In activities where productivity cannot be increased, a 33 per cent rise in staffing levels – and thus in the payroll – would be required when working hours are reduced by a quarter (to a thirty-hour week). The relative price of services where productivity is stagnant would tend to become exorbitant by comparison with the prices of many industrial products, which are continuing to fall. It must be a prime concern to compensate the wage loss due to shorter hours in a way which does not entail such a distortion of the price system. The solution to this problem will be to let direct wages be reduced as working hours diminish, and to compensate this reduction by an indirect income paid out of a separate public or semi-public fund, on the model of social benefits. For working hours reduced, for example, by 12 per cent, direct wages would be 12 per cent less than they otherwise would have been, but the employees would receive a "second cheque" – to use Guy Aznar's felicitous expression – of 12 per cent.[3] The RWH would not, therefore, increase the cost prices of low-productivity activities, though one might imagine this wage compensation being modulated in such a way as to exclude activities of no social utility (e.g. gaming establishments, personal servants, luxury hotels). Obviously, those performing artisanal activities and services paid for on a job-by-job basis would also be entitled to a second cheque, paid at the "going rate".

The second cheque cannot be financed by contributions taken from income. That would amount to taking back with one hand what had been given with the other. It cannot be financed by a tax on productivity gains, either ("making the machines pay", as the slogan goes): this would amount to having everyone's second cheque paid by the enterprises which make efforts to raise their productivity. They would surely see no reason to keep putting themselves to such pains if the tax system robbed them of the advantages that might be derived. The financing of the second cheque must therefore be fiscally neutral, both for enterprises and for working people. Only one kind of tax can meet this twofold condition in the long term, and that is a tax on consumption, in the form either of VAT or of specific taxes (on fuel, motor vehicles, luxuries, alcohol, etc.). This mode of financing will, in the long term, have the added advantage of raising the prices of those industrial products whose cost prices are falling rapidly, but whose increased consumption would not be in the interests of society or individuals, or the conservation of the environment. In the shorter term, it is self-evident that it will be possible to finance the second cheque to a large extent by means of a partial reallocation of unemployment benefits.

Obviously, one may envisage more complex formulas, as do the German Greens or Bernard Guibert, combining income from work and a basic social income payable to all citizens. The chief feature of the German formula is that a "binomial" monthly income should be paid, made up of a fixed amount of about £405 plus the normal income for twenty hours of weekly work. Bernard Guibert's formula proposes a tripartite income, including a universal allowance (or "wage for citizenship") and earnings linked to the quantity and quality of work performed. I believe, however, that the second cheque corresponding to the price of the work which no longer needs to be performed will initially be the most attractive formula.

How are Incomes and Jobs to be Redistributed?

The most complex problem is not, however, that of financing; it concerns the redistribution of the fruits of productivity and growth by way of RWH, extra jobs and wage increases. It is not sufficient merely for the legislators to decide an RWH of 10 per cent, for example, for the level of employment to increase automatically by 6 per cent and the level of pay by 2 per cent, as in scenario A 4. That scenario will never be brought about with mathematical precision. The number of jobs created will always be less than 6 per cent. For "households", having more time at their disposal, will tend to buy fewer services from professional providers, and the RWH will also speed up the growth in productivity per hour, if only by reducing absenteeism.

It is practically impossible, therefore, to forecast the rise in productivity with total accuracy, and select a corresponding RWH. But the impossibility of doing this is far from negative in its implications: it demonstrates that the economy and the society cannot be managed on purely technocratic lines, and that the choice of an RWH will always *initially* be a political decision. It is this which must be regarded as an independent variable. It is up to the economy to adapt itself to this, just as it adapted to the Sunday rest day, the eight-hour day, the forty-hour week, paid holidays, and so forth.

However, RWH will be translated into a net creation of jobs only if work and incomes can be redistributed from activities where high productivity gains can be made to those in which productivity rises slowly or not at all. That redistribution will be possible only if, for the various types of activity, their growth (or decline) and the development of their productivity can be forecast approximately. Only on this condition will it be possible to orientate workers towards jobs which the RWH will make available when it comes into force.

WHO IS IRREPLACEABLE?

Except in the rare case of the "creative genius", a person who is irreplaceable is so only for a limited period. Someone considered indispensable at a particular moment can normally be replaced by another after a period of training and familiarization. Indeed, it is the duty of a coherent democracy to expedite such possibilities of substitution by encouraging access to skills for all, and thus to reject rigidities and fixed patterns in the division of social tasks.

JEAN-BAPTISTE DE FOUCAULD, *La fin du social-colbertisme,*
Paris 1988.

These forecasts cannot, however, be purely statistical. The economy is not a machine which operates in a rigorously determinist fashion. It is the outcome of projects, intentions and programmes. The quality of forecasts and adjustments depends on the translation of the intentions and projects into commitments, contracts, collective agreements at branch and enterprise level. This contractualization has many more advantages than disadvantages (as is evident from the Swedish example in particular). By its mere existence, it reduces uncertainty and produces predictability. Plans and commitments made for several years are, in any case, a necessity for the public services and administrative bodies which have to plan their investments and staffing levels several years in advance. The same is true for most "capital-intensive" enterprises. The task of a planning body consists precisely in bringing together and harmonizing sectoral plans, and directing overall general development towards the priority goals set by government. Forecasting, dialogue, harmonization and orientation have a regulative, stabilizing effect once they are translated into contractual commitments.

However, a contractualization of this kind cannot remain confined to agreements at the top. It will have real impact only if, from the point where the date is set for the implementation of RWH, the trade unions and the users' and consumers' associations rightfully participate, at all levels, in working out the prognoses, plans and overall priorities. This will enlarge the competence of trade unions in a way which has long been advocated in Italy and is beginning to be argued for in Germany and Great Britain, in the name of that "economic democracy" that has been in all the programmes of the European Left parties for forty years or more.

It is, in fact, impossible to foresee how the structure and level of employment, production priorities, productivity and skills will develop without collective bargaining at branch and enterprise level on the nature and consequences of future technical changes, the modalities of their introduction, the training programmes that will be required, and the changes of skills, working conditions and relations, hours of work, productivity and staffing levels.

It is one of the specific aims of an RWH policy to render such collective bargaining necessary. At enterprise and branch level, there must be collective agreements extending over more than a single year and including productivity contracts and contracts relating to staffing levels. Announcing several years in advance that working hours will be substantially reduced at a set date is an extraordinarily effective lever for mobilizing society for what is simultaneously a challenge, an opportunity, a goal and a springboard towards new changes. The stakes for the workers and the interest they can take in this are far more stimulating than anything quality circles have to offer. All the aspects of working conditions are now up for grabs. "How will your workshop, office or department operate with an average working week of thirty-five hours (or thirty-two or thirty)? What changes in working hours or in your work station do you think are necessary in the light of the technical changes that are coming? And so on." The "workers' right to self-expression" will assume its full meaning in the context of these discussions and negotiations. Clearly, they presuppose strong trade unions. But, conversely, it is from these discussions and negotiations that the trade unions will draw their strength, as the Swedes, the German metalworkers and the Italians in the CGIL have reason to know.

WIDENING THE SCOPE
OF NEGOTIATIONS

The problems which have to be mastered if working hours are to be reduced are too immense and too numerous to be treated in any other way than by wide-ranging negotiations between all the social partners, negotiations carried on simultaneously at several different levels.

The important thing is to negotiate on the concrete forms the reduction will take, on the productivity and organization of work (particularly machine running hours), on the development of wage and social costs, and on the timetable for the creation of new jobs.

At the national level, all this implies an invitation to negotiate issued by the government, the establishment of basic guidelines and, then, the

---

conclusion of an interprofessional agreement. The aim of that agreement would be to lay down a general framework within which the social partners would be encouraged to conduct negotiations with a dynamic perspective . . .

Ultimately, it is at the level of weekly hours of work and through enterprise-by-enterprise negotiation that one must proceed, to examine on a case-by-case basis how to maintain machine running time, reorganize work, adapt incomes to the changed situation, create new jobs and avoid a deterioration in working conditions. . . . This presupposes more powerful and better-organized trade unions and managing directors who are prepared to negotiate, and debate on matters which they currently regard as theirs alone to decide. Ultimately, a further step forward in the transformation of industrial relations, such as was begun between 1969 and 1972, has to be achieved.

Échanges et Projets, *La révolution du temps choisi.*
Preface by Jacques Delors, Paris 1980.

Of the many questions which still remain to be answered, I shall deal here only with two which relate to problems that arise whenever there is change by stages.

1. When the RWH comes into force, extra jobs will become available. These will have to be filled by unemployed people who have received the appropriate training or retraining. This does not, however, solve the problem of those enterprises where productivity is growing at a rate equal to or higher than the planned RWH. Before this comes into force, these enterprises will be overstaffed, returning to normal levels only on implementation of RWH. What will they do with a personnel which, at the end of the period, will exceed their needs by, say, 10 per cent? The answer is relatively clear: the staff will be entitled to a training of their choice for a number of hours which increases as the implementation date for RWH approaches. These hours of (professional, artistic, manual, psychological or medical) training will represent a kind of "advance" against the coming extension of free time, and will prepare them for it. Whether their payment in full for these hours should be met by the "second cheque" or by the enterprises themselves, for which wages generally represent only a small fraction of unit costs, is a question I leave open.

FOR A NEW CONCEPTION
OF TRADE UNIONISM

We need a political and social project which enables us to bring together all the strata who have an interest in positive social change, but also recognizes the aspirations of the new social subjects. The challenge unions must face up to concerns their ability to put those objectives which are capable of uniting all dependent workers – both working and unemployed – at the centre of the class struggle ...

To this end, we must offer the marginalized strata new forms of organization which enable them to participate and become mobilized in action, forms which prefigure a horizontal structuring of democracy and unions.

The organization of leagues of unemployed youth within unions could be one solution. But there are other possible ventures, particularly all the forms of action and association by which young people cannot only demand but themselves create a new relationship between school and work: by deciding the training programmes and the content of the work themselves, and by themselves undertaking to provide services in the public interest ...

In no case must these be regarded as *satellite* organizations of the traditional labour movement. The new forms of organization will contribute to the unity of the dependent workers only if they are combined with a transformation of the current organizations of the working class. What is required in reality is a change in the nature of the trade union itself, and a fundamentally new conception of its role. This is what is needed if the unions are to show that they reject the idea of becoming an association of "sheltered" workers, and are not content just to represent those workers who have steady jobs ...

The unions, industrial unions and their horizontal structures must, in the neighbourhoods, towns and regions, promote "structures of movement" which organize all the forces of the unemployed, the casually employed, and working students *within* the union, to enable these people to have an effective say, from the inside, in the formulation of overall trade-union policy in both the industrial unions and the zonal councils ...

Extract from *Il Sindicato dei Consigli* (Rome 1980) by Bruno Trentin, current general secretary of the CGIL.

2. In the period preceding the RWH, the resources that are to be made available, when the time arrives, for creating extra jobs must not be used to pay the existing workforce. Levels of payment cannot, therefore, rise as quickly as they would without an RWH with net creation of jobs. To achieve such a moderation or limitation of wage rises, there

is no need to limit the scope of collective bargaining in an authoritarian manner. In any event, authoritarian attempts to restrain trade-union autonomy have never been successful in the long term. The moderation of wage claims will, rather, be the product of the trade unions' decision progressively to include within the scope of their bargaining those people who are not yet employed, and who are being prepared to occupy the jobs which the RWH will make available. In other words, *those waiting to take up jobs have to be involved in trade-union life and collective bargaining.* Negotiations must be extended to cover their rights, their pay and the nature and length of their training. I leave open the question of how these trainees who will receive a job when RWH is implemented are to be paid – whether this should be from the usual social benefits, by the "second cheque" and/or from contributions paid by employers and employees. The same rules and proportions do not necessarily have to apply in all branches.

Thus I am not proposing a limitation of the trade unions' bargaining power but, on the contrary, a *trade-union policy* on economic, fiscal and employment matters, on social priorities, on the model of consumption, the quality of life and the environment. This enhancement of the scope of trade-union activity is necessary if trade unions are not merely to degenerate into mutual aid societies for the well-to-do, and if industrial struggles at enterprise and industry level are to have more than merely sectional interests at their base. Far from paralysing trade unionism in an institutional role, trade-union policy can, as I have just demonstrated, extend the workers' control over the whole field of working conditions.

Notes

1. This is a reworking of an article published in October 1989 in *Partage*, the monthly paper of the unemployed workers' union. After the unification of the two Germanies, the text was updated and published in September 1990 as a supplement to the three publications of the Sozialistisches Büro and, subsequently, in *Neue Gesellschaft/Frankfurter Hefte* 11, 1990.

2. See Guy Roustang, *L'emploi: un choix de société*, Paris 1987.

3. See Guy Aznar, *Le travail c'est fini et c'est une bonne nouvelle*, Paris 1990.

Will There Be a European Left? Theoretical and Political Queries

Otto Kallscheuer

> Never let yourself be goaded into taking seriously problems
> about words and their meanings. What must be taken seri-
> ously are questions about facts, and assertions about facts;
> theories and hypotheses; the problems they solve; and the
> problems they raise.
>
> KARL R. POPPER[1]

> We speak about Social Democracy all the time, but Social
> Democracy is exclusively a European problem, which exists
> neither in the USA nor in the Third World.
>
> NORBERTO BOBBIO[2]

1. After the collapse of (un)"real socialism" in the East, should we still go on normatively characterizing the tasks of a radically libertarian Left as "socialist", and referring to them politically by that term? Even in the West, this venerable adjective fell victim to hyperinflation long ago. Perhaps this is merely one of those terminological quibbles against which the liberal Viennese freemason Dr Simon Siegmund Carl Popper warned his little son – at such an early stage that the younger Popper remained a critical rationalist for the rest of his life.

If André Gorz wants to retain this term today – though without holding on to the idea of socialism as a "*system*" – he certainly does not do so merely for reasons of nostalgia. There are at least two political "questions of fact"* he can muster against the sceptics: (a) the necessary Left critique of *Communism* (not just of the bureaucratic political system and authoritarian parties of that name, but also of the "ideal" communism of the young Marx and the "praxis philosophy" tradition); and (b) the critique of the social-democratic welfare state, a critique which is essential to the future of social solidarity. The libertarian critic of actually existing capitalism and its actually existing Left parties, who no longer sees the adjective "socialist" as having any relevance, will still have to confront these issues.

(a) The term "communism" can no longer be used to describe the goal of a just society, since it now carries with it the memory of the Marxian Romantic utopia of a "positive supersession" of *all* alienation (via the supersession of private property as the highest stage of the self-alienation of the human species). Ideal communism is a community without any autonomous social agencies of co-ordination and integration: when he was coining the term "*communisme*" in 1842, Étienne Cabet remained unsure for a long time whether he should not in fact prefer "*communité*".

As is well known, for the young Marx the "true appropriation of the human essence through and for man" is accomplished as "the complete restoration of man to himself as a social, i.e. human being, a restoration which has become conscious and which takes place within the entire wealth of previous periods of development",[3] in so far as the rupture between individuals and social institutions (private property and the market in the *Economic and Philosophic Manuscripts*, state and bureaucracy in a *Contribution to the Critique of Hegel's Philosophy of Right*[4]) is completely superseded only by way of this *return* to the lost paradise. The ideal-communist "communitary society" [*Gemeinschaftsgesellschaft*], as Gorz calls it in this book, realizes a conception of the *essence* of the human being, of the dream of philosophers: consequently, it is no longer the horizon of activity of individuals in the plural, each one of whom is unique. Any idea of "man as such", no matter how it is formulated, argues Hannah Arendt (and the same existentialist impulse informs all of André Gorz's work), implicitly contradicts the possibility of action: "Plurality is the condition of human action because we are all the same, that is, human, in such a way that nobody is ever the same as anyone else who ever lived, lives or will live."[5] Exit communism.

(b) Nevertheless, neither can a modern Left's demands for justice in

---

* *Translator's note*: In English in the original.

CAPITALISM, SOCIALISM, ECOLOGY

society be satisfied by the social-democratic welfare state, for the simple reason that this is itself a product of the decay of sociality [*Gesellschaftlichkeit*]. Regulation by the social state – necessary as it still may be for want of anything better – creates no social solidarity, but compensates for social decay, arising from (and constantly reproduced by) "asocial socialization" in the world of consumption.

We see, on the one hand, the allocation of normal welfare-state transfers and payments to the employed worker-consumers and salaried middle classes and, on the other, the "social question" constituted by an uninsured (de-classed or immigrant) new proletariat which is hived off on to bureaucratically administered social security authorities or asylum departments. But this differentiation within the system of welfare-state support is itself merely a replication in administrative terms of the notorious "two-thirds" society. The various classes of social poverty are ranked in descending order on the basis of their relationship to the work-based society's central category of the fully and permanently employed. Provision and classification by the welfare state no longer allows even that "*abstract*" form of relations of solidarity to arise among the citizens and inhabitants of our societies which Jürgen Habermas[6] (in contrast to the *concretist* version of community relations of solidarity) sees embodied, as an "intersubjectively shared expectation", in the inclusive mechanism of opinion- and will-formation in constitutional, democratic states.

The social-bureaucratic "regulation of poverty"[7] has, rather, the effect of breaking down solidarity by amplifying isolated individuals' fears of downward mobility. Anyone who has ever witnessed the different treatment meted out to skilled workers who can be relocated, "those capable of retraining (and willing to do so)", "those difficult to place", "older and long-term unemployed" and other "social cases" in an employment office (and *below these* there is still the negative hierarchy of foreign job-seekers, asylum seekers, and so on) knows from experience: the social or welfare state contributes to the increasing scarcity of the "resource of solidarity".

Where to now? Is socialism still a useful signpost? True, the term has a fine tradition, since it contains within it after all, the word *societas*, society. Socialist comes from *socius*, comrade, partner, member of a society; the term therefore derives simultaneously from Catholic natural law and the self-help of the early workers' associations. Should, then, the struggle for the reintroduction of a social dimension of communication and of control over the autonomous steering mechanisms of market and bureaucracy (and against them) be called "socialist"? Even though, today, the term socialism "as a comprehensive structural formula for an order of society . . . is operatively empty" (Claus Offe[8])?

To me the name appears altogether secondary.* And yet, in the democratic battle of ideas, it can hardly be a matter of indifference to the Left, whether its corporate identity "catches on" in the political marketplace. That is why, were I a politician (which I am not), it would be no problem for me to jettison the term entirely and, like the ex-Communists in Italy, simply revert to the untrammelled concept of the democratic Left, as a catch-all term for those men and women who are pro-democracy and who (within democracy) "champion the cause of those disadvantaged under existing conditions". The Italian postmodernist philosopher Gianni Vattimo has even suggested that "this programmatic 'poverty' [of a Left defining itself by the modest reference to democracy and social justice] might be an advantage, if it . . . thereby becomes possible to take up the problems and yearnings for emancipation of those social groups which, even today, feel excluded from full citizen rights – groups which still make up a considerable proportion of our society".[9]

2. I have much greater difficulties with the (singular) noun, the "*social movement*", than with the adjective "socialist", at least in the sense of a normative, positively invested (self-)characterization of what are, in fact, fairly heterogeneous "eco-social" forces for reform.[10] Admittedly, the concept of the social movement did not originate with the modern social question and the parties and trade unions of the skilled working class, but it none the less acquired its historico-political definition in the

---

Here André Gorz puts the following counter-questions:
Can one simply ignore the fact that we live in capitalist societies – indeed, in a capitalist world economic system? And that capitalism continues to reign supreme, even though what Claus Offe says about the term socialism equally applies to it: namely, that as a "comprehensive structural formula for an order of society, . . . [it] is operatively empty"? Can we forget that socialism defines itself as the antithesis of capitalism – that is, as the radical critique of forms of society in which the imperative of capital valorization shapes power relations, decision-making, models of development and consumption, technology, work and everyday culture? Does not writing off the reference to socialism also lead to abandoning every reference to a world beyond capitalism that is to be gained, to accepting capitalism as "natural" and "final", and to philosophizing in naively idealist terms about democracy and justice, while the economic-material core of violence, oppression and exclusion which are inseparable from capitalism, from the predominance of economic rationality, are dismissed as secondary?
As long as no other term is available to designate the emancipatory overcoming of capitalism the reference to (a nevertheless redefined) socialism must in my opinion be retained.
Jürgen Habermas similarly argues that socialism as "radically reformist self-critique of capitalist society . . . will disappear only with the object of its critique" – that is, "when the society in question has changed its identity so much that it allows the full significance of everything that cannot be expressed as a price to be perceived and taken seriously" (Habermas, "What Does Socialism Mean Today?", p. 21).

conflict between labour and capital:[11] that is, in the context of a socioculturally identifiable (and self-identifying) collective actor in the central conflict of capitalist industrial societies.

But is this term "social movement" (in the singular) adequate today to describe a multiplicity of forms of mobilization, protest and action on social, ecological and civil rights issues, which are underpinned by a host of contradictory interests and interpretations? For all the multipolar actors and conflicts which are supposed to be promoting, hastening or initiating a democratic, social and ecological transformation of our societies?[12] There are, indeed, many movements (and many other groupings which aspire to become movements), but does the *one* social movement, *the* alliance of the labour movement and the "new social movements", exist?

Would it not make more sense, therefore, to describe such a combination of quite contradictory sectional forces from the outset as a political social compact, as a reform process initiated, perhaps, by extra-parliamentary mobilization or, at any rate, by the formation of public opinion, but ultimately deriving its legitimacy from the building of a democratic majority? It would then be the task of the particular political "Left" to bring about these changing coalitions of movements, opinions and reforms. (And this would also turn the term "Left" back from a political shibboleth into a relative concept: relative to the specific tasks of reform, and relative to the various forces of inertia – or even reaction – in play.)[13]

There are not only theoretical reasons for my mistrust of the concept of movement in the singular (in any case, it is itself a classic acceleration concept from the semantic arsenal of the prophets of progress) but also political ones, related to the experience of the various protest *movements* in West Germany since the 1970s. For the rhetoric of movement always needs one enemy – a social adversary. This was the case with the labour movement: admittedly, its social adversary, the capitalist class, was *not* identical with the systemic logic of the capitalist economy, against which the social meaning of the struggles of the labour movement was directed, but it was a plausible – and in early capitalism by no means historically unjustified – simplification to understand and conduct the struggle for the shortening of the working day as a conflict of "right against right" (Marx[14]) between two parties – the working class and the industrial capitalists.

True, this conflict was as a rule decided (and displaced: from the struggle for socialization to the struggle for an incomes policy and the welfare state[15]) by shifting coalitions with the third party to the conflict – the state. And, for that very reason, the struggle for universal suffrage had a primordial place in the struggles of the old social movement.

In the majority of modernization conflicts in contemporary capitalist industrial societies, however, the field of battle and the opposing parties are no longer so clearly visible at a glance. And this is certainly difficult for the subjects who form part of the various "movements" to cope with, not just cognitively but also emotionally. Consequently, the diverse and changing sectional movements (or politically: the various fractions of the Left) look again and again for a "principal contradiction", the *one* (class or species) enemy, *against* whom all efforts must be united, concentrated or "focused". But this, presumably, makes sense only if one can reduce the adversary to a collective *subject*: for example, "big capital", "the" techno-fascistic new ruling class of multinational capital or (lately in Germany) "the *Treuhand*"* or the like . . .

Indeed, the longing for an identifiable enemy can be heard only too often in the political rhetoric and propaganda of part of the "autonomous movements" or of their spokespersons. It mostly displays an elective affinity with that Green or autonomous fundamentalism which Gorz rightly and eloquently criticizes.[16] Such a concept of a movement, or such a self-conception, which to some extent has a semantically built-in pattern of *constant radicalization* (quite appropriate for individual conflicts and mobilizations), usually functions, however, in Manichaean terms, as the absolute dividing line between "us" (good) and "the enemy": intermediate forces are put down (according to the old logic of "Social Fascism theory") as especially subtle attacks by the opposition (and combated with particular vehemence). There is no room for ambivalence!

The antagonistic movement–institution opposition leaves no place for the pursuit of *political reforms* of the kind Gorz rightly calls for, mediating between, on the one hand, the established coalitions and interests within the industrial system, and, on the other, post-industrial forms of society and ecological imperatives. For even the project of "shorter working hours as a social contract" can no longer be understood as a struggle of the old labour movement against the employers (and that movement will inevitably lose its historical identity as a consequence).

Gorz himself writes of the field of conflict, in which disputes over the ethical, social and political limits of economic rationality[17] are fought out, having become "multidimensional". The protagonists change; not all are involved in the same arenas. And not all can straightforwardly be classified as "part of movements". (I am thinking, for example, of the "movement entrepreneurs", who are much more common in the American ecology and consumer movements; or, in the Federal Republic, of the highly

---

Translator's note: The government agency responsible for privatizing state industry in what was the GDR.

professionalized counter-experts in various eco-institutes, who by way of mixed funding – from the Energy Ministry among others – float a report in the research market, which, with appropriate media connections, gets this or that megaproject talked about and then – at the next election – shot down.) What sense does it make here still to talk of *one*, albeit "multi-dimensional", social movement?

3. Modern societies are no longer integrated by *one* action co-ordination mechanism, but by at least three: market regulation, political power, consensus[18] – and presumably particular account should also be taken today of the academic and research business as a largely autonomous subsystem. For Gorz, too, the autonomy or "alienation" of the social subsystems from all cognitive and lifeworld-practical control by the individual, which inevitably results, can never be fully removed – and this is *a fortiori* the case, as he demonstrated in detail in *Critique of Economic Reason*, under the conditions of a functionally differentiated division of labour.

Such a supersession of alienation (or overall de-differentiation of social subsystems) would, anyway, not even be desirable. After all, it is precisely in pre-modern, functionally undifferentiated societies that the ontological (or existential) non-identity between each particular subject-individual – who is irreducible to any other in the living of his or her *own* life – and his or her *social* identity (Gorz: "the identity which society obliges him – or gives him the means – to express")[19] is permanently overpowered by natural communitary bonds; in traditional social organization, this "split within the subject" with regard to his or her social being, a split which is constitutive of individual autonomy, is, as a rule, prevented or at least checked by individuals being organically ascribed to corporations or to naturally ordained "estates" that are part of a social body in which religious, political and economical determinations all coincide.

To put it the other way round: precisely the modern "differentiation of roles" between *myself* as employee/consumer/taxpayer, *myself* as citizen and *myself* as member of a football or pigeon fanciers' club and, on the other hand, *myself* as (in all these roles) an individual *with a mind of my own* endowed with reason and emotion, grants me additional space for thinking and acting in (and against) each of these roles, without pinning me down to any one of them.[20] Role differentiation is itself the result of a secular process by which individuals have been liberated from organic community ties. Paradise lost.* In Paradise, it was forbidden to

---

*Translator's note: In English in the original.

think for oneself: the very first presumptuous act, the tasting of the fruit of the Tree of Knowledge and passion, led to expulsion. The original sin of freedom.

In a complex society, therefore, none of three (or four or more) interacting subsystems can determine (or "colonize") social relations without the whole dynamic of the society unavoidably being harmed, and losing the capacity for adaptation and learning. But, even more importantly, every *monocratic* hegemony or predominance of one of the socially relevant spheres of action limits the freedom of individuals to shape an autonomous life, which, in the form of a separation from the public sphere of a particular, private space for living, is part of the *"liberté des modernes"* (Benjamin Constant). The recognition (and defence) of a "separation of powers" between diverse, contrary, and, in their "specific logic", autonomous spheres of rationality – in other words, the dissolution of monopoly formations in the regulation of the social structure of action – constitutes, therefore, a *liberal* inheritance, beyond which no modern Left (or "socialist") programme may relapse with impunity.

It is possible to understand this Left and (in an American sense) liberal tradition in Ronald Dworkin's or Michael Walzer's[21] terms "as an 'instrument' to block and combat the tyrannical use of power" – of *every* power, indeed, not least that of the market. In this sense a pure market society (where the economic power of the market is the sole and general criterion for the distribution of economic, political and cultural resources), in which the economic position of a person alone determines access to the vote, to education, to work and leisure, to love and affection, social recognition, protection against sickness and need, would as much have to be combated as a tyranny as would the rule of a bureaucratic *nomenclatura* (in which position in the hierarchy is the only relevant distribution code) or of a fundamentalist theocracy (in which orthodoxy determines how well – or badly – one fares). Such a "market imperialism", the imperialism of economic reason, would contradict the ideals of freedom and equality just as much as a totalitarian socialism or the socially normative dictatorship of a state religion.

The diverse nature of the various fronts and aspects of – and actors in – the "central conflict" over the direction, extent and forms of social modernization which are sketched out here does not exclude the possibility of conferring a "potential meaning" on development or, in other words, of seeing this in terms of a "logic" (a self-intensifying mechanism) of the reform and reconstruction of industrial society. Gorz is right: it is a question of transmuting the liberation of time and individuals into new *civil rights and liberties*. These embody the "potential meaning" of social development, and represent the political tasks of a libertarian Left.

Yet this process of extending freedom simultaneously requires the social learning of self-limitation – self-limitation on the part of the individual and the self-limitation of the automatic process of social rationalization. "Modernity" (like "Progress" or the "Movement") is now no longer an unequivocal source of hope or an unqualified concept of liberation. It is becoming ambivalent, becoming a terrain of conflicts over the form, extent and direction of social modernization. And, by way of these conflicts over second-order modernization problems, it is also becoming the terrain of social alternatives. The term "reflexive modernization", introduced into social philosophy by Ulrich Beck – the notion of reflexively interrupted progress – implies precisely this.

The fact is that we cannot abandon the "cognitive compulsion to progress" (Wolfgang Krohn) – that is, cannot abandon going back over our own behavioural rules, modes of knowledge and value judgements in a process of *self-reflection* – or, at least, we should not want to. Not only is it a feature of the maturity of our modernity (and not only of modernity, for there are classical and Christian versions), but no satisfactory development beyond – or exit from – modernity is conceivable without reflexive *self-correction*. And this reflexive "feeding back in" of the critique of progress can indeed be regarded as the most advanced – and even the most intense – form of progress. But it means parting company with the previously accepted model of the course of scientific, technical and social progress: the model of linear acceleration or "headlong flight forward". Reflexive modernization requires an ethical, social and ecological *self-limitation*, which may be more reminiscent of classical values of *care of the self*[22] than of the modern heroic quest for emancipation (even if it need not contradict the idea of emancipation – reflexively inflected).

- "Modernity" can, on the one hand, be understood as the ruthless *emancipation of the rationalization process* (the separating out of the subsystems of science, economics and administration) from the limits imposed by the moral economies of the community. In that case, it would be necessary to reduce or avoid this functional differentiation, so as to reflexively tie it back in.

- But on the other hand, "modernity" can also be understood as *emancipation of individuals* (and of the democratic community) *from the religion of economic rationality*, from the constraints of work-based, industrial society. In that case, its normative content would hardly have been thematized yet – because leaving behind industrialist immaturity would require of us the capacity for self-limitation, and above all require the "restriction of the scope of economic reason".

In sociological terminology, this would mean the reduction (*not* the complete removal) of external control by autonomous systemic forces, by introducing social "reflexivity" into all individual systems of activity (economics, politics, law, social communication and interest-formation, sciences), if we are to be at all able to address and negotiate "second-order modernization problems". "Social, political and economic systems of action can certainly be reconstructed" – writes Claus Offe –

> in such a way that their protagonists are induced to reflect on the long-term effects of actions, or the burden of proof of the tenability of action is placed upon them, and, on the other hand, that they are freed from direct dependence on the pre-given standards of other systems of action.... The common basic idea is to reconstruct social systems in such a way that they burden their environment less with problems and at the same time themselves become more autonomous in relation to their environment, as a result of which it is on the whole possible to expect a reduction in co-ordination problems and control requirements".[23]

To refer now concretely to the conflict between working hours and time for living, André Gorz's proposals for a post-industrial social contract[24] are fully consonant with this perspective, as for example when:

1. it is stated that the political framework for the *reduction in working hours* (which, though decided at the level of society as a whole, is to be flexibly applied in individual plants, depending upon their type of work organization and/or the available increases in productivity) *is to be discussed in the plants themselves* (as are the specific trade-offs in terms of hours worked and wages received);

2. a combination of social basic income (however defined) and greater control over their own work are to enable people to achieve a higher level of (freely determined) *self-sufficiency in the work they perform for themselves* as part of the organization of their own (private, family and community) lives, and so breathe new life into their currently stunted micro-social lifeworlds;

3. the hours that are freed up from (paid) work and the increased *satisfaction of social and private needs of a non-economic nature* are to render infinite expansion of the consumer goods market (with its attendant ecological costs) unnecessary.

Such a "multidimensional" social contract cannot by any means be shaped by the trade unions and employers alone, as in the "classical" model. It must be initiated by a radical public sphere (not least by the associations of the unemployed!), must be democratically accountable within the political system, and will therefore inevitably have to be negotiated by a great many different social actors and authorities. Its dynamic is no longer that of *la lutte finale*, the decisive battle between the armies of proletariat and bourgeoisie – between the universal class on the one side of the barricades and the usurpers of social wealth and their state lackeys on the other, even if there continue to be barricades and picket lines, civil disobedience and strikes in the struggle for civil liberties, social justice and quality of life.

And this, perhaps, is true to an even greater extent where questions of ecological rationality are concerned (as, for example, in the establishment of pollution limits, the assessment of risk and the "polluter must pay" principle) where there are *no* clearly pre-defined coalitions of interest (since the "species" has no interests). Admittedly, these concern public goods, but for the most part they are still not recognized as objects of legitimate and institutionalized conflict (as is still entirely the case with the classic "social" conflict themes of wages, working hours, social services). Political ecology's critique will have to apply itself practically in a jungle of constituted interests and (mis)interpretations – and there will be no possibility of starting out afresh from zero. A politics of ecological reform has to assert itself (1) against the standards of rationality – which must be respected even as they are being criticized – of the (necessarily) autonomous media of social control; (2) among particular dominant interests (and interest groups) and oppositional organizations and institutions (trade unions, environmental and consumer interests, for example); so as to be able to contribute to (3) reducing the participants' system-generated blind spots;[25] and (4) increasing the degree of social control of those directly affected; as well as (5) taking into consideration *not only* those affected, but also those indirectly involved, including future generations.... The accountability problem of ecological costs and the avoidance of ecological damage must also "be regulated by agreements achieved through conflict, *social contracts* and legal norms" (Ulrich Beck).

To put this another (and more concise) way: there is no longer a single, unambiguous *sociocultural* force which can act as a vehicle for effecting the necessary reconstruction of the industrial system. This depends, rather, on the power of public spheres to bring themes on to the agenda (or to block them) and, most importantly, on the creation of new *institutional* responsibilities for determining ecological causes and effects. Hence, there is much to be said for Ulrich Beck's surmise that "the question of the political subject in industrial, class society has its counterpart in risk society [*Risikogesellschaft*] in the question of *political reflexivity*".[26] However, in what Beck terms "risk society", the horizon of causes and effects, of damage and consequences, ceased long ago to be the nation-state.

4. Until the lifting of the Iron Curtain it was "only" the ecological ravages of industrialism which completely disregarded all state boundaries, including the frontier between East and West. The Chernobyl radioactive cloud or the acid rain from Czech or West German chimneys also harmed Italian vegetables and the romantic Black Forest. Yet the antagonism between the two blocs also served to provide welcome relief from the pressures of public opinion in the free world, as for example when West German toxic waste was disposed of in exchange for Deutschmarks in dumps in the "socialist" countries (whereas France, as a former colonial power, preferred to ship contaminated nuclear refuse overseas, or dump it at sea). With the end of communism in Eastern Europe, the social question has, in its turn, become Europe-wide. And it is how it is dealt with that will chiefly decide the *question of democracy*.

Only a few years ago Jiří Dienstbier, as one of the spokesmen of "Charter 77", was being persecuted and prevented from working by the Communist regime. Today he is Foreign Minister of Czechoslovakia,[*] and has become one of the figures who symbolizes the new urgency of the democratic question.[27] In January 1991 Dienstbier warned against the "disintegration of the East", against the "new democracies being suffocated by an economic collapse". A return to Europe? "If we are not able rapidly to create economic conditions in Central and Eastern Europe which give people at least the hope of a gradual improvement in their standard of living, and progress towards Western levels" – he writes – then this could "lead to a new totalitarianism or to dictatorships of various types".

The people's democracy of a new type (reminiscent in some respects of the "plebiscitary leadership democracy" analysed by Max Weber) already exists today in Romania and Serbia – and will exist tomorrow, perhaps, in Albania. If Western economic aid is inadequate, and Eastern Europe is not coupled sociopolitically to the Europe of the EC, Dienstbier predicts that political regression will take one of two forms: either the trend "towards a new division of Europe into rich and poor with the potential danger of totalitarianism or dictatorship in the future"; or, with a more favourable outcome, "these countries would become a constant source of refugees and emigrants to the West, and

---

[*] *Translator's note*: This was written before the election which brought conservatives to power and precipitated the separation of the Czech Republic and Slovakia. Dienstbier is a leading figure in the "Civic Movement" in the Czech Republic. It is not, however, represented in Parliament.

that would undermine Western societies and create new, dangerous animosities".[28] One hardly needs to add that the two trends need not be mutually exclusive, but may feed off one another. In fact, this is exactly what is happening at the moment.

Already "Europe" is no longer "Brussels". Europe has become a continent in motion – with a socioeconomic East–West drift into the wealthy countries of the European Community. It has long been a continent of immigration from the South; only Eastern Europe formed (almost) to the last an anti-migration protective wall for the democratic-capitalist nations between the Elbe and the Atlantic, even though this was already becoming porous. Yet nothing is at it was any more.

In the twenty-first century, there will no longer be Soviet tanks to prevent the mobility of people and ideas, of commodities and currencies. This is a role that has already fallen to the local police. And shortly there will (inevitably!) be citizen defence forces, popular militias – against Vietnamese and Africans in Leipzig or Hamburg; against North Africans in Marseille or Paris; against "Polish black-marketeers" in Berlin or against Pakistanis and West Indians in London; against "Albanian troublemakers" in Greater Serbia . . . and finally, all over Europe, against "thieving, Gipsy beggars".

"All those things that have always haunted imaginations behind the Iron Curtain" – writes the Berlin poet and essayist Bernd Wagner, who fell from East to West and was there overtaken by German unification – "now really do exist, more so than ever: rebellions, pogroms, wars and revolutions. Everyone is fighting everyone else again . . . Europe will have to learn to live with poverty again, as a constant threat, as a part of life. Europe is becoming one, the world is becoming one."[29]

The old continent has become *one* social, economic area of mobility, whose existing internal and external boundaries – in the ravines of the Balkans, on the wide plains of Russia, in the little harbours of the Mediterranean, in the Polish, Ethiopian, East Asian cheap charter flights – have long been porous. The national boundaries, the Customs, asylum and aliens departments, still exist, of course – the dark side of the internal welfare states, whose negative hierarchies they extend downwards. Yet without a definition of criteria and quotas, of residence and civil rights, which must be negotiated and enshrined in law at the European level, for the broken families and scattered groups in the (trans)continental currents of flight and migration, any particular state sovereignty is merely window-dressing for the precept that "might is right": the strong nation against the weak minority, the economically strong among the weak (who can pay for the lawyers and the bribes and can get round the system) against the weakest of the weak, the illegals, who are filtered out.

European unity is here now, but as state of nature, as a *bellum omnium contra omnes*. Without a "civilizing" of the transnational migrations – of the new, *continent-wide social question* – which satisfies the demands of human rights, national boundaries will degenerate into a vast black market. They will become filters for separating the poor from the rich, the settled worker-citizens from the foreign nomads, national groups possessing a state from persecuted or irredentist minorities (who then oppress their own minorities in turn).

Where does Europe end? At Brindisi, with the tide of Albanian boat people at its gates? Or on the Neisse, where German neo-fascist radicals, socialized by "real socialism", vent their hate on Poles entering visa-free (at last)? In Creil on the Oise, where the republican Bastille of the *école laïque* is defended against the Islamic masses in the shape of two Moroccan sisters wearing headscarves?[30] In the town halls of Berlin boroughs, where Soviet Jews, arriving via Tel Aviv, request admission and naturalization?

Where is Europe? What cultural, moral and political resources can the "European ideology"[31] call on? Right now, today, on the threshold of the post-industrial age, when the countries of Europe are confronted with the multinational poor from bankrupt early-industrialist development dictatorships? Will the Western Europe of the European Community become a fortress? Do the Europeans possess the capacity to handle the complexity, diversity and contradictoriness of their cultural codes productively and conflictually, but also democratically (Edgar Morin)?

Europe has been the birthplace of Caesaro-Papism (the Byzantine Empire) *and* of the separation of Church and state (investiture dispute*), of the Reformation *and* of the Inquisition, of the Enlightenment *and* of the Holy Alliance, of *raison d'état and* of human rights, of rationalism *and* of irrationalism, of capitalism *and* of socialism, of the "nation one and indivisible" *and* of the *ius cosmopoliticum*, of democracy *and* of totalitarianism, of the historicist philosophy of progress *and* of the Romantic critique of civilization. . . .

So what might a *cultural compromise* for the future of Europe look like? It would indeed have to avoid the reactionary "wrong track of the nation-state" (Peter Glotz) – the illusion of national sovereignty already overtaken both by the transnational integration of economies and societies and by the transcontinental mobility of people, commodities and ideas – yet it dare not advocate any ideal of *one* homogeneous European culture.

***Translator's note*: Dispute of the English, French and German monarchs with the Papacy over the investiture of bishops and abbots.

Libérer et fédérer. The simple thing that is so hard to do: "The demonstration of ethnic-cultural distinctiveness need not be counterposed to the recognition and validity of universal human and civil rights" (Claus Leggewie). Neither *"l'Europe des nations"* (de Gaulle), then, nor *"Nation Europa"* – the title of a radical right-wing racist paper. Neither "the new evangelization of Europe" (Pope Woytila) nor the path of segregation, of *cuius regio eius religio,** which leads to the logic of the state Church and the ghetto which leaves the question: *Europe, pour quoi faire?*

5. The collapse of the Eastern bloc has turned the continent of Europe into a *single* social space again. However, this space has not yet acquired any political structure, but is increasingly turning into institutional chaos – and so into a social and ecological trap. Since 1989 at least, it has been possible for the democratic, social, ecological and cultural questions to be dealt with responsibly – that is, effectively – only at a European level.

Yet that arena is empty: the parties of the Left which, before the fall of the German Wall, had frequently and volubly advocated the "Europeanization of Europe", also deserted the European stage after the Iron Curtain had been opened up, and gave themselves over primarily to their various national joys and fears. The morning after: the *Western* Europe of nations is celebrating a resurrection. The nations of Eastern Europe are abandoned to their old internal rivalries. Let the losers of the Cold War keep to themselves!

In the European Community, it is national governments and the heads of the central banks who decide on the prospects for political union – and its inevitable expansion to include the other half of Europe. And they have put it on the back burner. The Commission of the European Community and the Council of Ministers have proved reluctant to develop the European Parliament into a *legislature* deserving of the name – one that is not merely able (as in the latest proposal, of 17 April 1991, of the European Commission and the Council of Ministers) to exercise influence by means of a veto.

No concrete steps towards a joint European integration of the young and threatened East European democracies have yet been made. Indeed, quite to the contrary, bilateralism is once again in fashion, as though the Iron Curtain were still – or were back – in existence. What objection can there be, for example, to immediately setting up a *Joint European Environmental Agency* which, as a matter of course, would have

---

**Translator's note*: Formula of the Peace of Augsburg (1555), ordaining that the ruler of a territory should determine the faith of his subjects.

to be able to rescind "sovereign" economic and energy policy decisions? How long will it be before the international charter on civil and political rights which came into force in 1976 (and to which the Hungarian government appealed in 1989 when, in spite of the protests of the GDR government, it permitted the departure of thousands of GDR citizens, and so set the avalanche of liberation in motion) is given institutional embodiment?

Why has a code of European civil rights not even been agreed at EC level? This would presuppose the creation of a court for European civil law which was able, for example, to monitor and revise the asylum legislation of individual member countries. And – to return to the oldest and most venerable of the European parties of the Left – did not Nobel Peace Prize-winner Willy Brandt, as head of the Socialist International, say even before the "turning point" that only a Europe based on social and ecological reason could contribute in a new world economic order to a development policy of burden-sharing with the countries of the Third and Fourth Worlds threatened by global demographic and natural catastrophes, and thus rise above national egotism and social conservatism?

If, however, "the dramatic end of Communism in Europe ... caught the Left on the wrong foot", as Hermann Schwengel writes; and if, at the same time, "the relations between Europeanization and socialism have been anything but happy as yet",[32] then perhaps this is more than mere coincidence. For democratic socialism as the political formation of the social movement of the working classes[33] came into being – and has always seen itself – within the frame of the nation-state. On 4 August 1914, the internationalist proclamations of the Stuttgart Socialist Congress (1904) turned out to be not worth the paper they were printed on. The pioneers of a "reconstruction of Europe" (Eduard Bernstein[34]), who argued for the creation of a European "Federation of States" (Kautsky[35]) characterized by free trade and democracy, remained voices crying in the wilderness during and after the First World War.

And after the Second? The great, innovative figures of the European Left – Palmiro Togliatti, Bruno Kreisky, Willy Brandt – were not only *national* spokesmen in their own countries for the interests of the dependent classes; their foreign policy of advancing beyond the bipolar order "by small steps" also bore the stamp of a sense of national responsibility. This becomes even clearer when we look at those on the second rank of the party conference platforms, such as Egon Bahr, German Social Democracy's advocate of détente, and Giorgio Amendola, the Italian Communists' European specialist. Their shared limitations show through in their inability seriously to challenge the model of stability implicit in the economic and collective security policies of a "Europe of nations".[36]

For although the Soviet empire of greater Russian "socialism in one country" had, with its satellites, become the enemy of the West in the Cold War, for the great reformist parties of the European Left it none the less guaranteed that geopolitical stability which was the basis (though they never openly admitted it) on which they could conduct their national and socialist policies of defending the working classes. The welfare state and Keynesian incomes policies required not only economic predictability, but also a foreign policy that could operate with stable factors.

"Yalta" was also consolidated by the West European Left – in the interest of their national skilled working classes, with little or no regard for Solidarność or "Charter 77".[37] The only uncertain factor in the postwar order was the German question, which had become frozen with the Cold War. This, as we know, has now been solved. But does this mean we are any closer to a "European social space"? Up to the present, the party political Left in Germany has presented itself more as the national tribune of the people against the social "costs of unification" than as the avant-garde of a multidimensional social contract of freedom and justice transcending the nation-state.

6. Today the European nations are themselves experiencing "the American situation" for the first time – as a cultural and social question. Europe has become a continent of immigration, the borders are (not *de jure*, but *de facto*) open to competition for admission on the part of the strongest among the weak, just as the iron Tex-Mex curtain in the southern States of the USA does not prevent the illegal immigration of Mexican Latinos into "God's Own Country". In Europe, as in America, the "melting-pot" will not eradicate existing or incoming social, national, cultural and religious identities, but will increase their numbers and lead to permanent confrontation.[38]

In contrast to the USA, there is no United States of Europe, no common constitutional patriotism with regard to the rights and freedoms to be respected by all inhabitants. Nor is there the barbaric possibility of wiping the slate clean of the native peoples and cultures; for in Europe it is the natives, not the immigrants, who are strong. Shall we ever see a European Republic?

"Why is there no socialism in the United States?" asked Werner Sombart at the turn of the century. Let us turn the question around. Might it not be that European socialism, bearing the stamp of the nation-state, the context within which it arose when the labour movement developed from self-help associations into parties and trade unions,[39] is itself one of the barriers to the formation of a United States of Europe? A barrier to be removed, if we understand that term in a Hegelian sense, as *Aufhebung*, as simultaneous elimination, supersession and preservation.

And the trade unions? Despite their proclamations to the contrary, they too have *not* up to now shown themselves to be a unifying factor on the path to a single European social space. Is it by chance that within the "political class" of the Euro-Left, it is *not* a trade unionist but a European politician shaped by social-liberal and Christian traditions – Jacques Delors – who is responsible not only for the most radical "Brussels" proposals on political union, but also for the most radical reflections on the connections between the social question, the new poverty and innovative policies of control over working hours?[40]

To sum up: Are the new "American situation" of Europe and the old "genetic code" of European socialism compatible? Shall we see the civil Republic of Europe come about, if we continue to tie ourselves to the old and new skilled worker elites and their organizational "juggernauts" (Peter Glotz)? If the alternative is couched in these terms – *either* the socialist Left *or* an open Europe with civil rights – then a libertarian Left will decide *against* the *laager* of the working-class movement[41] and *for* the Federal Republic of Europe. Either – or.

I have, of course, deliberately exaggerated the situation. Is there really no third way? A third possibility does perhaps exist, though this is not a middle way, but a transformation of the Left itself. A Left which resolved to take on the "American situation" would, from the outset, have to apply the idea of the new social contract which André Gorz advances – along with the many social forms of negotiation by which ecological responsibility is, in Ulrich Beck's proposals, to be embodied in institutions – to the European space as a whole. There is no model and no home for such an "American Left"[42] in Europe. But there are many starting points – among the East European civil rights campaigners, among the Greens, among the Lafontaine wing of the Social Democrats, in the post-Communist Left both within and outside the ex-PCI, but also among Christian Democratic reformers like Heiner Geissler in Bonn, Kurt Biedenkopf in Leipzig or Leoluca Orlando in Palermo.

Its political tasks could be condensed in the old Resistance slogan *libérer et fédérer*. European federation has the "potential meaning" of extending guarantees of civil and social rights to *all* the inhabitants of democratic Europe, and setting these – by stages, of course, in a series of transitional phases – on a common legal basis.[43] If this course were to be taken, the social alliance Gorz writes of between the "modern skilled workers" and the post-industrial proletariat would have to be supplemented by negotiated immigration quotas and social minimum guarantees for immigrants[44] – that is, for that multinational "non-nation of the (as yet) non-possessors of civil rights" – the pariahs from the South and East.

*

7. *Encore un effort, citoyens!* Today, with the increase in trans-European migratory movements, the flow of economic and political refugees from the immediate periphery (North Africa, Turkey, Balkans, Eastern Europe and the Near East) and from the Third World is increasingly being superimposed on the distribution struggle within the boundaries of the nation-state (labour against capital, Ossies against Wessies, civil servants against taxpayers, and so on). Europe, as a continent of immigration, faces the following alternatives:

- It can, as André Gorz has put it, "South-Africanize" itself: in this case, each member of the "Europe of nations" would set up its own iron curtain against the growing demographic pressure from the East and South, and restrict civil rights to an "ethnically" defined nation. Inside, the trade unions would continue to fight for their share of GNP and against the black market of disenfranchised immigrants. Those who nevertheless inevitably slip through the meshes of the curtain would be relegated to second-class-citizen status, with no access to the labour market or welfare benefits. The colonial model of the servant classes and races and the inferior ranks would once again have a foothold in the heart of Europe.

- The alternative – the creation of Europe as an open "social space" – requires that a code of European civil rights be established which is not tainted by the national birthmarks of ethnicity, but provides "aliens" with access to both political and social rights (e.g. a guaranteed minimum income) on a non-discriminatory basis.

All social struggles are also disputes about the definition of "citizenship" – about rights and the real opportunities of access to employment, qualifications, the social system, and so on. In conditions of increased transnational mobility, according civil and social rights differentially on the basis of national identity leads to social conflicts being displaced on to inter-ethnic conflicts (and the pecking order here is already familiar to us from German reception camps: Germans–Poles–Turks–Coloureds, etc. ...). If conflicts over the social distribution of wealth at the end of the millennium are not to degenerate into ethnocentric protectionism on the part of the "Europe of nations", then the social question in Europe must become the question of civil rights for "aliens".

The demarcation between "citizens" and "aliens" thus turns into the question of a civil (and not national) definition of European citizenship itself. For both the definition of the "alien" and the way the "alien" is treated by the citizens depend on – and, reciprocally, influence – the character of the defining (discriminating and discriminatory) citizenry. When walls and barbed-wire fences are falling in Europe, a libertarian Left should insist that other criteria than ethnic character should hold sway in the Republic.

Translated by Martin Chalmers and Chris Turner

Notes

1. Sir Karl insists that he *developed* this "anti-essentialist" view at the age of fifteen in conversations with his father in Vienna. Karl Popper, *Unended Quest: An Intellectual Biography*, Glasgow 1976, p. 19.

2. "Die gefährdete Utopie der Demokratie", Peter Glotz and Otto Kallscheuer in conversation with Norberto Bobbio, *Die Neue Gesellschaft/Frankfurter Hefte* 10, 1989.

3. Karl Marx, *Economic and Philosophical Manuscripts (1844)*, in *Early Writings*, Harmondsworth and London 1975, p. 348.

4. The demand for the withering away of the state had already been formulated by Hegel in 1796 or 1797 in the *Älteste System-programm des deutschen Idealismus* [The Earliest System-Programme of German Idealism]: because "no idea of the state *exists*, because the state is something *mechanical*, and there is no idea of a *machine*. Only what is an object of *freedom* can be called an *idea*. So we too must go beyond the state!" In complete contrast to this Romantic devaluation of the mechanical – as opposed to the living community, loving "commune" [*Gemeinde*] or organic nation [*Volk*] – it was precisely the liberal enlightenment (beginning with Montesquieu) which saw in the neutral play of rules, the mechanism of checks and balances (the separation of powers) and the predictability of impartial legislation a possibility of freedom for individuals. That, in our actually existing democracies, without civic virtues and a sense of solidarity and public action, these possibilities must wither away is quite another matter (see Norberto Bobbio, *The Future of Democracy*, Cambridge 1987); it does not, however, contradict the fundamental gain in freedom constituted by the ("mechanical") separation of the state and civil society.

5. Hannah Arendt, *The Human Condition*, Chicago 1958, p. 8.

6. Jürgen Habermas, "What Does Socialism Mean Today? The Rectifying Revolution and the Need for New Thinking on the Left", *New Left Review* 183, September–October 1990.

7. Frances F. Piven and Richard A. Cloward, *Regulierung der Armut*, Frankfurt-am-Main 1977. The important introduction by Stephan Leibfried compares the welfare systems of the USA and the FRG. For a useful introduction to the Federal German "inverted net of social security" and its sociopsychological consequences, see Wolf Wagner, *Angst vor der Armut*, Berlin 1991.

8. In his contribution to the Habermas Festschrift, *Zwischenbetrachtungen*, Frankfurt-am-Main 1989, p. 746.

9. Gianni Vattimo, in his contribution to the debate on the name change of the Italian Communists in *La Stampa*.

10. On this theme see, for example, the contributions to "Zukunft der Reformpolitik", in *Forschungsjournal Neue Soziale Bewegungen* 1, 1991.

11. Werner Sombart's classic, *Socialism and the Social Movement in the 19th Century* (London 1909), can still be recommended.

12. One can add even more hyphenated adjectives: non-violent-feminist-convivial-anti-racist, etc. The piling up of adjectives could, however, be an index of the fact that we are no longer dealing with *one* movement at all, but with changing terrains and arenas, changing actors in the "central conflict" over how our societies are to be modernized.

13. See Hermann Schwengel's stimulating arguments: "Das zweite Leben des Sozialismus", *Die Neue Gesellschaft/Frankfurter Hefte* 6, 1990; "Soziale Frage – Demokratische Frage – Kulturelle Frage. Die drei politischen Welten der Marktwirtschaft", *Prokla* 89, 1991.

14. Karl Marx, *Capital*, vol. 1, chapter 10, Harmondsworth and London 1976.

15. See Adam Przeworski's outstanding sketch "Social Democracy as a Historical Phenomenon", *New Left Review* 122, July–August 1980.

16. See Chapter 1 above.

17. But surely also with regard to the limits of scientific, administrative and democratic rationality (for example, in the case of majority decisions on nuclear power stations). "Reflexive modernization" affects *all* modernity's patterns of rationality.

18. In the terminology of Charles E. Lindblom: exchange, authority and persuasion. Charles E. Lindblom, *Politics and Markets: The World's Political-Economic Systems*, New York 1977; Jürgen Habermas talks of the "three resources money, power and solidarity" ("What Does Socialism Mean Today?").

19. See, in *Critique of Economic Reason* (London 1989), André Gorz's remarks on the concept of "lifeworld": "The Limits of Sociology and Socialization. A Digression on the Notion of the Lifeworld", pp. 173–80.

20. See the fine excursus "Über den Begriff der Ehre und seinen Niedergang", in Peter L. Berger, Brigitte Berger and Hansfried Kellner, *Das Unbehagen in der Modernität*, Frankfurt-am-Main 1973, p. 75. One can also turn to the older classics: "The positing of the individual ... in this nakedness is itself a product of history", writes Marx in one of his great disgressions on social theory in the draft for *Capital* (*Grundrisse*, Harmondsworth and London 1973, p. 472; instead of the " ... ", Marx of course writes "as a *worker*"). This release of the individual from the pre-given bonds of traditional communities, which appeared to their members as – in Marx's words – "natural conditions of existence", this *increase in contingency*, must in modern societies be "mastered" by each individual in the construction of his or her personal identity. But, along with a progressive functional differentiation of society, it is the basis also of the "counter-modernizing" search for (old or new) community formations (Berger, Berger and Kellner, *Das Unbehagen in der Modernität*, p. 155). If it is not "civilized", then the striving for re-union [*re-ligio*] is a source of – among other things – religious "fundamentalism", especially in situations of social crisis.

21. See Michael Walzer, *Kritik und Gemeinsinn*, Berlin 1990.

22. See Pierre Hadot, *Exercices spirituels et philosophie antique*, Paris 1981.

23. Claus Offe, "Die Utopie der Null-Option. Modernität und Modernisierung als politische Gütekriterien", in P. Koslowski, R. Spaemann and R. Löw (eds), *Moderne oder Postmoderne*, Weinheim 1986, p. 168.

24. See Chapter 9 above; *Critique of Economic Reason*, Part III and Appendix ("Summary for Trade Unionists and Other Left Activists").

25. Systemic blindnesses – the screening out or misjudgement of vital boundary conditions and knock-on effects – such as repeatedly occur, especially in decisions on technology policy, *may*, but *need not*, be interest-induced (see Jon Elster, "Belief, Bias and Ideology", Part IV of *Sour Grapes: Studies in the Subversion of Rationality*, Cambridge 1983, pp. 141–66). In Marxian terms, "false consciousness" and "dominant ideology" (in the sense of serving the dominant interests) are by no means necessarily identical. It is also possible to do the wrong thing for good reasons (or in the interest of just, generalizable goals), particularly since (with modernity) we have become dependent on the autonomous subsystem of science for our knowledge of the boundary conditions, knock-on and long-term effects of every decision; but also because decisions can never be postponed until we have assembled complete information on all the relevant interests, circumstances and consequences. The condition of *total* information for decisions and actions is an impossibility for humans as finite living and reasoning beings (only an omniscient God could rescue us from this *condition humaine*); that is why the demand for the greatest degree of re-examination of collective decisions (here, too, nothing *total* is possible) is not only a democratic, but also an ecological imperative.

26. Ulrich Beck, "Die Grünen in der Weltrisikogesellschaft", in Ralf Fücks (ed.), *Sind die Grünen noch zu retten?* Reinbek 1991, p. 191. See also U. Beck, *Politik in der Risikogesellschaft*, Frankfurt-am-Main 1991.

27. Within the West German Left, the renewed relevance of the democratic question (too long suppressed) has been pointed up again since the collapse of the communist states by Ulrich Rödel, Günter Frankenberg and Helmut Dubiel, *Die demokratische Frage*, Frankfurt-am-Main 1989; Thomas Schmid, *Staatsbegräbnis. Von ziviler Gesellschaft*, Berlin 1990. For a discussion between Western and Eastern analysts and protagonists, which is fertile precisely because of the contrasts which emerge, see the contributions to the first issue of *Transit. Europäische Revue*, 1990: "Osteuropa – Übergänge zur Demokratie?"

28. Jiří Dienstbier, *Träumen von Europa*, with a foreword by Václav Havel, Berlin 1991, p. 185. (Afterword 1991: "Vom Träumen zur Realität".)

29. Bernd Wagner, *Die Wut im Koffer. Kalamazonische Reden*. Berlin 1991, p. 271.

30. See on this question (and for what follows) Claus Leggewie, *multi kulti. Spielregeln für die Vielvölkerrepublik*, Berlin 1990, pp. 74–87.

31. For a brilliant defence, enlightened yet sceptical, of the universalist contents of European culture, see Norberto Bobbio, "Grösse und Verfall der europäischen Ideologie", *Lettre International* [Berlin] 1, Summer 1988. Of course the future, "potential meaning" (Gorz) of this European inheritance lies with those "Rights of Man and the Citizen", which were historical in their develop-

ment and reality but universal in their implications, and whose legally effective diffusion across the globe and successive "generations" represent for Bobbio the pre-eminent "indicators of historical progress". Bobbio distinguishes between four "generations" of human rights which arise out of and correspond to the great conflicts or movements of modern times: (1) the classic basic freedoms and political civil rights; (2) social civil rights; (3) the heterogeneous category of consumer rights, rights to ecological quality of life and data-protection, behind which is already emerging the new generation; (4) that of the right to protection from the manipulation of the genetic inheritance: N. Bobbio, *L'età dei diritti*, Turin 1990.

32. Schwengel, "Das zweite Leben des Sozialismus".

33. See Przeworski, "Social Democracy as a Historical Phenomenon".

34. Eduard Bernstein, *Sozialdemokratische Völkerpolitik*, Leipzig 1917.

35. Karl Kautsky, *Nationalstaat, imperialistischer Staat und Staatenbund*, Nuremberg 1915.

36. In order to understand the implicitly national-neutralist aims of Egon Bahr's "new *Ostpolitik*", a reading of his book *Zum europäischen Frieden. Eine Antwort auf Gorbatschow* (Berlin 1988), is recommended. With this social-democratic diplomat one must, however, also read between the lines (think always of German unification, never talk about it!; see Arnulf Baring in the *Frankfurter Allgemeine Zeitung*, 28 March 1988). On the national limits of the long-serving faction leader of the PCI in the European Parliament, Giorgio Amendola, the great champion of the Italian Communist "Right", see the excellent (self-)critical contribution by Umberto Minopoli and Umberto Ranieri, "Il riformismo dopo il PCI", *Micro-Mega* 1, 1991.

37. See Adam Michnik's appeal to Willy Brandt, "Entre la Russie et l'Allemagne", in *La deuxième révolution*, Paris 1990, pp. 177–94.

38. On this subject, see the stimulating theses which Étienne Balibar presented at the congress on "Migration and Racism in Europe" (Hamburg, 27–30 September 1990). Translated into English as "*Es gibt keinen Staat in Europa*: Racism and Politics in Europe Today", *New Left Review* 186, March–April 1991.

39. And when the Syndicalist Left had to learn "that the normal professional party of the European worker is different in its essence from revolutionary Marxism". Arthur Rosenberg, *Democracy and Socialism*, Boston, MA 1965.

40. Jacques Delors, *Our Europe*, London 1992. See also Chapters 7 and 9 above.

41. See Peter Glotz, *Manifest für eine Neue Europäische Linke*, Berlin 1985.

42. There is, in addition, in France the fondly cherished negative image which Gaullist Marxists (Jean-Pierre Chevènement or Régis Debray, for example) like to present of a *gauche américaine*: a "third" Left which is neither communist nor socialist but simultaneously technocratic and libertarian.

43. See, as a preliminary attempt at formulation, the "Charta der politischen, sozialen und kulturellen Rechte der Minoritäten und Flüchtlinge in der Europäischen Föderation" by Claus Leggewie in *multi kulti*, pp. 160 ff.

44. Not only would this mean the macro-economic aspects of the eco-social contract inevitably becoming (to put it mildly) considerably more complicated;

I suspect also that the right of immigrants to move freely and compete *legally* within the European labour market will have the effect of diminishing the importance of the opposition, on which Gorz lays such emphasis, between a "liberal" and a "socialist" variant of the right to a basic income, with or without a right (or duty) to work. To misappropriate a phrase of Claus Offe's: it will be more important to guarantee a European minimum than to achieve national maximums. It would seem to me, from a universalist standpoint, more important to introduce the "liberal" measure of a guaranteed minimum income for immigrants, combined with civil rights and the right to seek employment, than to achieve the "socialist" variant of a guaranteed income for life linked to a specific quantity of work to be performed over that lifetime. The contradiction between equality before the law and social inequality would not, of course, be resolved by such a measure: it would merely secure a space in which it could be fought out and publicly negotiated.

Gorz makes the following comments on these observations:

If the increase in the total workforce is to be regulated by immigration criteria and quotas "negotiated at the European level" (which I accept), why should this make "the macro-economic aspects ... considerably more complicated"? Can European immigration quotas be anything other than the sum of the foreseeable regional capacities to admit migrants? In order to guarantee immigrants not just the formal right but also the real *possibility* of "mov[ing] freely and compet[ing] *legally* within the European labour market" (again, accepted), does this not mean that the development of the market, of productivity and of the skills required, must be planned at enterprise, industry and regional level, and a corresponding policy of vocational training and work redistribution implemented? Or, my dear friends Otto and Claus, do you envisage a neo-Liberal, Friedmannite policy with the sweeping away of all collective wage agreements and social insurance measures in favour of a guaranteed minimum income, in order that immigrants may find work, in an entirely de-regulated labour market, by bypassing the (disempowered) trade unions and undercutting the wages of the "local" workers.

Why do you take the view that immigrants would be entitled only to "minimum guarantees"? Why shouldn't they receive the full incomes I envisage here in Chapter 9. Why shouldn't the social contract guaranteeing a full income during the periodic interruptions of waged employment and in retirement also apply to immigrants. And why shouldn't they take part in the collective bargaining process? Who would gain from the fact of only minimums being guaranteed, and the whole dynamic of distribution struggles, collective bargaining and the effort to expand the contractual social net *as far as possible* being halted? Are you not, perhaps, forgetting that this is still a capitalist society, that the antagonism between labour and capital still remains, even when the trade unions have grown bureaucratic and the working class in the advanced industries has become corporatist and conservative? And that the reduction of all guarantees to a minimum would only increase the rate of profit, the power of capital and its room for manoeuvre? Possible European minimums will always depend on national minimums *and maximums* – that is, on the balance of social forces.

Finally – to quote Kant – one should always defend utopia (i.e. the norm of the greatest possible equity) against those who base themselves on what currently exists. To do otherwise is to become mere *miglioristi*, to be content simply to improve what exists, and thereby lose the capacity to make a fundamental critique.

Index

Radical Thinkers ▼

André Gorz
Capitalism, Socialism, Ecology
Critique of Economic Reason

Max Horkheimer
Critique of Instrumental Reason

Fredric Jameson
Brecht and Method
The Cultural Turn
Late Marxism
A Singular Modernity

Karl Korsch
Marxism and Philosophy

Ernesto Laclau
Contingency, Hegemony,
*   Universality*
Emancipation(s)
Politics and Ideology in
*   Marxist Theory*

Henri Lefebvre
Introduction to Modernity

Georg Lukács
Lenin

Herbert Marcuse
A Study on Authority

Franco Moretti
Signs Taken for Wonders

Chantal Mouffe
The Democratic Paradox
The Return of the Political

Antonio Negri
The Political Descartes

Peter Osborne
The Politics of Time

Jacques Rancière
On the Shores of Politics

Wilhelm Reich
Sex-Pol

Gillian Rose
Hegel Contra Sociology

Jacqueline Rose
Sexuality in the Field of Vision

Kristin Ross
The Emergence of Social Space

Jean-Paul Sartre
Between Existentialism and Marxism
War Diaries

Edward W. Soja
Postmodern Geographies

Sebastiano Timpanaro
Freudian Slip

Göran Therborn
What Does the Ruling Class Do
*   When It Rules?*

Paul Virilio
The Information Bomb
Open Sky
Strategy of Deception
War and Cinema

V. N. Voloshinov
Freudianism

Immanuel Wallerstein
Race, Nation, Class

Raymond Williams
Culture and Materialism
Politics of Modernism

Slavoj Žižek
Contingency, Hegemony,
*   Universality*
For They Know Not What They Do
The Indivisible Remainder
The Metastases of Enjoyment
Welcome to the Desert of the Real

Alenka Zupančič
Ethics of the Real

Printed in the United States
by Baker & Taylor Publisher Services